FREEDOM FROM TOXIC RELATIONSHIPS

STRESS-FREE STEPS TO RECOGNIZING
GASLIGHTING AND CODEPENDENCY, REBUILD
SELF-WORTH, AND DEVELOP HEALTHY
RELATIONSHIPS, EVEN IF YOU HAVE TRIED
BEFORE

PIPER MADISON

CONTENTS

INTRODUCTION

How often do you question the health of your relationships? Each of our relationships impacts our life, adding to it or subtracting from our experiences. In the case of the latter, do you ever wonder how much of your self-worth is compromised by the dynamics you endure daily? These toxic relationships are more than just difficult interactions; they chip away at our core, leaving us feeling less than we are. This book will look at how to break free from the cycle.

Today, the urgency to address toxic relationships is undeniable. We live in a world where connections should uplift and support us. Life can be challenging with so many moving parts. Too many suffer silently in bonds that do nothing but undermine their lives. My journey into the labyrinth of toxic relationships began with personal experiences—navigating through the fog of confusion and self-doubt and emerging with a clearer understanding of what it means to love and be loved healthily.

This book is born from a deep desire to empower you. It aims to guide you through recognizing signs of toxic relationships, stepping away safely if that is your ultimate choice, and healing from the scars left behind. We aim to strengthen and rebuild yourself and foster nurturing relationships rather than depleting you.

What sets this book apart is its blend of personal insights backed by professional advice and practical, actionable steps that you can apply immediately. Taking a few minutes daily to work on your peace is worth it. Each chapter takes you on a journey of self-awareness, confrontation, healing, and growth, providing a clear roadmap to navigate this challenging landscape of relationships.

As we embark on this journey together, let this be a place of hope, empowerment, and transformation in your life. Let it be a turning point where you shed relationships that hinder your happiness. I am here to share knowledge and offer a space where you feel understood and supported. The emphasis on self-awareness, self-care, and personal growth weaves through the fabric of each page, aiming to lift you from the shadows of doubt and into the light of self-assurance and healthy relational bonds.

"The human spirit is stronger than anything that can happen to it." This powerful quote reminds us that despite our adversity, our spirit remains invincible, capable of overcoming and thriving.

You are not just reading a book but stepping into a life where your relationships enrich, empower, and reflect the true you. Let this be your guide to not only escaping the grip of toxic interactions but also embarking on a journey toward profound self-discovery, healing, and a life filled with abundant, healthy, loving relationships.

CHAPTER 1
UNDERSTANDING TOXIC RELATIONSHIPS

Have you ever stopped to consider the true nature of your relationships? It is a question that many of us might shy away from, especially if the reflection leads us down a road less traveled—one that involves confronting uncomfortable truths about the people we have chosen to surround ourselves with. Life is fast-paced, and we often do not stop to think about or even question some relationships that could negatively impact our life experience. This chapter focuses on what makes a relationship toxic versus just challenging. It is designed to help you discern the subtle yet significant differences that can impact everything from your self-esteem to your day-to-day happiness.

1.1 Defining Toxic Relationships: More Than Just Bad Days

Toxic relationships fundamentally differ from everyday conflicts arising from misunderstandings or momentary disagreements. These relationships, particularly, leave us feeling drained. While all relationships endure ups and downs, toxic relationships are characterized by enduring patterns of behavior that systematically undermine one's sense of well-being. These are not just bad days but persistent behaviors that erode trust, respect, and health.

One of the most precise indicators of a toxic relationship is persistent disrespect. This could manifest as frequent criticism, belittling comments, or actions that consistently make you feel undervalued or ashamed. Lack of empathy is another red flag; a partner or friend who consistently shows an inability or unwillingness to understand your feelings or viewpoints can create a hostile environment. Demonstrating manipulative behaviors are also telltale signs, where one person uses emotional blackmail, guilt, or gaslighting to control or influence your actions. This can leave you feeling confused about life and the relationship itself.

The impact of such toxic dynamics is profound. On a mental health level, it can lead to chronic stress, anxiety, and depression. Physically, the constant stress may manifest as insomnia, headaches, or other stress-related ailments. Socially, toxic relationships often lead to isolation, either because the toxic individual monopolizes your time or because their behavior drives other loved ones away, which is the beginning of isolation. They are breaking you from your support system, which is meant to provide a solid system of checks and balances for your health and well-being.

Contrasting these traits with those found in healthy relationships can further illuminate the differences. Healthy relationships leave you feeling good and nourished versus bad and depleted. Healthy relationships are built on mutual respect, where both parties value each other's opinions and feelings. Communication is open and positive, aiming to build up rather than tear down. Support in a healthy relationship is evident, with each person cheering on the other's successes and providing comfort during failures, fostering an environment where both individuals can thrive.

Reflective Exercise

To help you internalize the differences between toxic and healthy relationships, take a moment to reflect on your current relationships. Consider the following questions in your journal:

1. Do I feel respected by this person?
2. Are my thoughts and feelings valued and considered?
3. How do I feel after interacting with this person—drained or uplifted?
4. Is there a balance of give and take in our interactions?

This exercise is not just about identifying toxic traits but also affirming the positive aspects of your relationships that are worth nurturing and growing. By reflecting on these questions, you begin to draw boundaries between what is acceptable and detrimental to your well-being. Recognizing the signs is the first step towards fostering healthier connections and reclaiming your mental and emotional space.

1.2 The Spectrum of Toxicity: From Neglect to Abuse

When we talk about toxic relationships, it is crucial to understand that toxicity does not always present itself in loud, dramatic outbursts. Sometimes, the quiet, almost invisible behaviors gradually erode our sense of self and security. Think of toxicity on a spectrum where, at one end, there lies subtle neglect and, at the other, overt abuse. Each point on this spectrum can significantly impact individuals, albeit differently.

On this spectrum, we will start with neglect, which might seem less obvious but can be just as damaging to a sense of self. Emotional neglect in a relationship often manifests as a consistent failure to respond to your emotional needs. It might look like indifference to your feelings, overlooking your happiness and well-being, or consistently prioritizing their needs without considering yours. This behavior can leave you feeling undervalued and unheard. Imagine you are going through a tough time at work, and every time you try to discuss your challenges, your partner changes the subject, dismisses your concerns, or does not acknowledge what you are expressing at all, and minimizes your feelings. The absence of support and understanding speaks volumes here, leaving you feeling isolated and undervalued. This kind of neglect, particularly when chronic, can lead to significant emotional and psychological distress as the foundation of mutual support in a relationship erodes.

On the more severe end of the spectrum lies abuse, which can be broken down into several categories, including emotional, physical, and digital abuse. Emotional abuse might involve manipulation tactics such as gaslighting, where the abuser denies your reality, making you question your memories or sanity. Physical abuse is perhaps the most recognizable form, characterized by any form of violence or bodily harm inflicted onto one partner by another. Digital abuse, increasingly recognized in our connected age, involves using technology to control, harass, or intimidate a partner. This could include persistent text messages, emails, or even using GPS location to monitor a partner's whereabouts.

Each form of abuse not only impacts the individual's mental and physical health but also their ability to function in other areas of life. Victims may find it difficult to maintain other healthy relationships, perform at work, or engage in social activities, often due to anxiety, depression, or low self-esteem that these toxic behaviors foster. Moreover, the fear and stress caused by anticipating the next outburst or controlling behavior can make daily functioning a challenge, perpetuating a cycle of abuse and helplessness.

Understanding this spectrum is vital not just for recognizing the various forms of toxicity that might be affecting you or someone you know but also for appreciating the different levels of impact they can have. Early recognition of these signs can be the first step in seeking help, beginning the healing process, or ending the relationship. Awareness equips you with the knowledge to protect yourself and others from further harm, fostering environments where healthy, supportive relationships can thrive.

1.3 Common Traits of Toxic Partners and Friends

Recognizing toxic traits in relationships is crucial for maintaining your emotional health. We often encounter individuals who, unbeknownst to us initially, carry traits that can transform a seemingly healthy relationship into a draining and damaging ordeal. Understanding these traits—narcissism, control, jealousy, and unpredictability—is the first step in safeguarding ourselves against the potential harm they can cause.

Narcissism is marked by an inflated sense of one's importance and a deep need for excessive attention and admiration. Contrary to the self-confidence facade, deep down, narcissists struggle with fragile self-esteem and are highly vulnerable to the slightest criticism. Imagine a friend who constantly shifts every conversation to themselves, dismisses your achievements, or belittles your problems, making you feel invisible in the relationship. This behavior saps your emotional energy and can lead you to question your worth in the relationship.

Control in toxic relationships manifests through behaviors where one person consistently dictates the terms of the interaction, often disregarding the needs and boundaries of the other. A controlling partner might limit your social interactions and make decisions about how you should act, dress, or even express yourself, essentially stripping away your autonomy. For instance, if your partner insists on having passwords on all your digital devices to keep "tabs" on you, all under the guise of caring for you, this overstepping is a classic sign of controlling behavior and ultimately can undermine the relationship.

While occasionally natural in relationships, jealousy becomes toxic when it is pervasive and baseless. It can lead to possessive behaviors, with the jealous individual demanding constant reassurance or reacting negatively to your interaction with others. This can slowly isolate you from the other relationships in your life. An example might look like a friend who gets upset whenever you make new friends or acquaintances, interpreting this as threatening their relationship with you, leading to a stifling and oppressive environment.

Unpredictability in someone's behavior can create a sense of perpetual unease. One day, they may be warm and loving and, without apparent reason, become cold and distant the next. This can cause confusion on which version you will get to interact with today. This unpredictability is often used as a psychological tool to keep you off-balance and more likely to concede to their desires and demands out of your desperation to regain the 'good' version of them.

These traits often stem from deeper psychological issues. Narcissism, for example, might be rooted in a profound sense of insecurity or a childhood where the individual's emotional needs were not met. Control could be a response to previous situations where the person felt helpless or powerless; thus, they overcompensate by exerting control over others to avoid those feelings. Jealousy might originate from past betrayals or abandonment, and unpredictability could be a learned behavior from an environment where such mood swings were used as coping mechanisms.

Interacting with individuals who display these traits requires a strategy centered on solid boundaries. Establishing and maintaining firm boundaries is not about changing the other person—that is often beyond your control—but about protecting yourself. Fences make good neighbors; the same is true for boundaries; they are meant to enhance our relationships, not deter us from them. Suppose you have a relationship where your boundaries feel tested, then this may be something to examine more closely. You must communicate your boundaries clearly and consistently, without room for ambiguity. For example, if a friend exhibits jealousy, you might need to assert that while you value their friendship, you also value your freedom to form and maintain other relationships. In cases of control or manipulation, it might be necessary to seek external support, whether from other friends, family, or professional help, to reinforce your boundaries and ensure your autonomy is respected. Often, you can change your boundaries, which can impact your relationships. At other times, professional help is the best route because they can guide you through difficult times.

Navigating these dynamics also involves a degree of self-reflection. Understanding why you might be a target for such behaviors can be enlightening. People with high empathy and low conflict thresholds often find themselves in such relationships because they are naturally more accommodating. In recognizing these traits in yourself, you can better prepare to interact with those who may, whether consciously or subconsciously, seek to exploit these qualities.

In conclusion, while we cannot change other people's intrinsic traits, we can equip ourselves with the knowledge and tools to recognize and manage how we interact with them. Changing how we react helps maintain our mental and emotional health and empowers us to build and nurture healthier, more fulfilling relationships.

1.4 Psychological Underpinnings of Toxic Dynamics

Understanding the psychological foundations of toxic relationships is pivotal in both recognizing and addressing them effectively. From the clinical perspectives provided by attachment theory to the more dynamically observed cycles of abuse and trauma bonding, these frameworks offer profound insights into why and how these damaging relationships form and persist. Attachment theory, initially developed by John Bowlby and Mary Ainsworth, explains how early relationships with caregivers set the stage for future interpersonal dynamics. This theory delineates various attachment styles—secure, anxious, avoidant, and disorganized—influencing how individuals relate to others in their adult lives. Those with an anxious or avoidant attachment style may find themselves repeatedly drawn into toxic relationships due to their underlying expectations about love and worthiness. For instance, someone with an anxious attachment might tolerate excessive negativity or control because their early experiences taught them that such dynamics are synonymous with love.

Expanding on this, the cycle of abuse formulated by Lenore Walker in the 1970s provides a lens through which to view the repetitive patterns often seen in abusive relationships. This cycle includes four phases: tension building, incident, reconciliation, and calm. The predictability of this cycle creates a psychologically binding rhythm where, post-conflict, the abuser's apologetic behavior (reconciliation phase) rekindles hope for change, only for the cycle to repeat itself tragically. This cycle can be exceptionally disorienting and emotionally exhausting, making it difficult for individuals to leave the relationship due to the intermittent reinforcement of hope and love during the reconciliation and calm phases.

Trauma bonding further complicates the dynamic. This concept refers to the strong emotional attachment that develops between a victim and an abuser formed through the cycle of abuse. These bonds are cemented by the intensity of the highs and lows, with the positive reinforcement of affection following abuse fostering a powerful emotional connection to the abuser. It is similar to Stockholm syndrome, where hostages develop a psychological alliance with their captors as a survival strategy during captivity. In the context of a relationship, the victim often becomes emotionally dependent on the abuser, equating the relief from abuse and the sporadic doses of affection they receive as genuine care and love.

The role of self-esteem in these dynamics cannot be overstated. Individuals with diminished self-esteem are particularly susceptible to the advances of toxic partners who initially may present themselves as affirming and validating. Over time, these toxic individuals exploit their partner's low self-esteem, perhaps convincing them that they are to blame for the abusive dynamics or that they are incapable of being loved by anyone else. This manipulation serves to tether the victim more tightly to the relationship, as their sense of self-worth becomes increasingly reliant on their partner's fluctuating approval and acceptance.

Addressing these deeply ingrained issues begins with developing psychological awareness. Recognizing the signs of unhealthy attachment styles, the phases of the abuse cycle, and the nature of trauma bonding can empower individuals to seek help. Furthermore, bolstering one's self-esteem through therapy, supportive relationships, and personal development work is crucial. Engaging in self-care practices can serve as preventive and reparative measures, helping individuals build a solid internal foundation to withstand challenges in toxic relationships.

The journey toward healing from and avoiding toxic relationships is deeply personal and often challenging, necessitating a multifaceted approach that includes emotional education, personal reflection, and professional guidance. As we continue to explore these dynamics, remember that understanding the psychological underpinnings is not just about navigating away from negativity but also steering toward healthier, more fulfilling relationships that enhance our well-being and enrich our lives.

1.5 Why Toxic Relationships are Often Overlooked

In the intricate dance of human relationships, toxic dynamics can often be misinterpreted or overlooked, woven subtly into the fabric of our daily interactions. This oversight is not merely a personal failure but is deeply rooted in broader societal norms and cultural contexts that can normalize and even romanticize harmful behaviors. Society often portrays intense, all-consuming relationships as the epitome of romantic success, masking the underlying toxicity with a veneer of passionate love. This portrayal can lead individuals to misinterpret controlling or jealous behaviors as signs of deep affection, thereby normalizing a partner's oppressive tendencies. Moreover, cultural narratives around commitment and loyalty can pressure individuals to stay in unhealthy relationships under the guise of upholding family or societal values. Many individuals will remain in a toxic relationship because they think it is easier than leaving one.

This societal backdrop plays a crucial role in how individuals perceive their relationships. In many cultures, discussing relationship problems outside the home is frowned upon, reinforcing a cycle of silence and endurance. The stigma associated with breaking relationships, especially marriages, can lead individuals to tolerate toxic behaviors far longer than they might in a more supportive environment. The fear of societal judgment often weighs heavily, influencing decisions to stay in unhealthy situations out of a misplaced sense of duty or fear of ostracization.

Adding a personal layer to these societal pressures is the profound fear of loneliness many experience when facing the prospect of leaving a toxic relationship. This fear is not just about being alone but about confronting the void the relationship fills, even if negatively. Emotional dependency develops when one's sense of worth and emotional stability is intricately tied to one's partner, regardless of the toxicity present. This dependency is compounded by the fear of the unknown—of who one might be outside the confines of the relationship. It is akin to staying in a familiar, albeit harsh, climate rather than venturing into unpredictable weather despite the promise of clearer skies.

Moreover, there is a pervasive lack of awareness about what constitutes a toxic relationship. Without a clear understanding, many might not recognize the signs, especially when the toxicity creeps in gradually, cloaked in the guise of intense love or care. It is easy to dismiss concerns when you do not have the vocabulary to name what you are experiencing or when those around you downplay your concerns. Education about relationship dynamics often focuses on more overt forms of abuse, leaving those experiencing subtler forms of manipulation and control without the tools to identify and articulate their experiences. This gap in awareness can lead to a normalization of discomfort, where feelings of unhappiness or unease in a relationship are dismissed as everyday challenges couples face.

Signs of this normalization are evident when serious issues are consistently joked about or dismissed. Phrases like "That's just how they are" or "All couples fight" can minimize the impact of toxic behaviors, making them seem like standard elements of a relationship. Similarly, intense conflict might be misinterpreted as passion, with volatile interactions seen as evidence of a deep, albeit tumultuous, love. Such interpretations prevent a clear assessment of the relationship's health, skewing perceptions to favor staying over leaving.

Recognizing these signs and understanding the broader social and personal dynamics contributing to overlooking toxic relationships are crucial steps in changing how individuals and societies respond to them. It involves a shift towards greater awareness, openness in discussing relationship health, and a critical examination of the cultural narratives that shape our understanding of love and commitment. By addressing these issues directly, individuals can begin to distinguish between passion and toxicity, between enduring love and harmful dependency, and ultimately, make empowered choices about their relationships and lives.

CHAPTER 2
RECOGNIZING GASLIGHTING AND MANIPULATIVE BEHAVIORS

H ave you ever left a conversation feeling disoriented, questioning your memory or sanity? This unsettling experience, far from being a simple misunderstanding, might actually be the result of a psychological manipulation technique known as gaslighting. This chapter delves into the intricacies of gaslighting, a covert form of emotional abuse that can undermine your sense of reality and significantly impact your mental health. By understanding how to recognize and respond to gaslighting, you can protect your psychological well-being and reclaim your personal truth.

2.1 Gaslighting 101: An Introduction to Mental Manipulation

Gaslighting is a form of psychological manipulation where a person or a group covertly sows seeds of doubt in a targeted individual, making them question their own memory, perception, or judgment, often evoking in them cognitive dissonance and other changes, including low self-esteem. The term originates from the 1938 play "Gas Light" and its 1944 film adaptation, where a husband manipulates small elements of his wife's environment to make her believe she is losing her sanity. This manipulative tactic is not limited to personal relationships but can occur in professional settings and broader societal interactions.

The primary goal of a gaslighter is to gain power and control. By undermining your perception of reality, they place themselves in a position to dictate your emotions and actions, making you more dependent on them for the 'correct' interpretation of your experiences. This dependency allows the gaslighter to advance their own agenda, from avoiding accountability to maintaining a façade of competence or hiding nefarious activities. For example, if confronted about wrongdoing, a gaslighter might counter by questioning the reliability of your claims or your memory of events, shifting the focus and blame away from themselves.

Common phrases you might hear from a gaslighter include dismissals such as "You're overreacting" or denials like "I never said that." These phrases are often used to doubt your reactions or recall of events, respectively. They serve the gaslighter's purpose to confuse you and make you question your instincts and perceptions, which would typically guide your reactions and decisions.

The psychological impact on victims of gaslighting can be profound. The persistent doubt sewn into the fabric of your interactions can lead to a significant reduction in your ability to trust your own memories and perceptions, resulting in confusion, anxiety, and a diminished sense of reality. Over time, this can escalate into more severe psychological effects, such as depression and isolation, as you gradually lose confidence in your ability to discern truth from manipulation. This erosion of self-trust can affect various aspects of your life, including your relationships with others, your performance at work, and your willingness to engage in new experiences.

Reflective Exercise: Identifying Gaslighting

To better understand how gaslighting might affect your life, consider reflecting on recent conversations or interactions that left you confused or doubting your perspective. Write down the details of these interactions, focusing on what was said and how you reacted internally. Ask yourself:

- Did I feel confused about my recollection of events after speaking with someone?
- Were phrases like "You're imagining things" or "You're too sensitive" used?
- How often do I feel this way with this person?

This exercise can help you pinpoint patterns that suggest gaslighting, equipping you with the knowledge to address and rectify these dynamics in your relationships. Recognizing gaslighting is the first step in reclaiming your reality and restoring your trust in your perceptions and judgments.

2.2 Subtle Signs of Gaslighting in Daily Interactions

Gaslighting does not always wave a glaring red flag in the nuanced dance of human interactions. Sometimes, its signals are quiet, insidious, and incredibly easy to miss, especially when they are woven into the fabric of our everyday conversations and behaviors. Recognizing these subtle cues requires a keen sense of awareness and understanding that gaslighting can be as slight as a misleading comment or a small shift in a story that plants seeds of doubt about your perception or memory.

Consider a scenario where a partner questions your decisions repeatedly but in a manner that seems to come from a place of concern. For instance, if you decide to spend an evening with friends, your partner might say something like, "Are you sure you should go out? You know you have a busy day tomorrow, and I wouldn't want you to overextend yourself." This appears considerate on the surface, but if such comments are persistent, they can subtly undermine your confidence in your decision-making. Another common subtle tactic is gradually altering details in shared stories or events. Over time, these small changes can distort your memory of events, making you doubt your recollection and rely more heavily on the other person's version of reality.

The emotional responses elicited by these subtle forms of gaslighting are crucial indicators. Often, they manifest as feelings of confusion or a sense that you are losing your grip on reality, commonly described as feeling 'crazy.' You might question why simple interactions leave you unsettled or feel less confident about your memory or judgment after speaking with a particular person. These feelings are significant red flags, signaling that your perceptions are being challenged and that you might be the target of gaslighting.

In such situations, external validation becomes an invaluable tool. Maintaining a personal journal where you can document interactions and how they made you feel can help preserve a record of events as you perceived them at the moment, which is helpful for cross-referencing reality when doubt creeps in. Consulting trusted friends or family members about your experiences can also provide an outside perspective that affirms your reality or points out discrepancies you might have missed. This external input is essential in helping you distinguish between genuine memory lapses and instances of being manipulated through gaslighting.

The subtlety of gaslighting makes it a particularly dangerous form of manipulation because it can be easily rationalized or overlooked. This allows it to be embedded deeply in relationships and significantly impact mental health. By staying vigilant about the signs and trusting your feelings during interactions, you equip yourself with the tools to identify and address gaslighting, reinforcing your confidence in your perceptions and decisions. This vigilance is your first line of defense, enabling you to maintain your mental clarity and sense of truth in the face of subtle manipulation.

2.3 Differentiating Manipulation from Misunderstanding

Navigating the complexities of human interactions often requires us to discern between genuine misunderstandings and intentional manipulation. This differentiation is crucial as it influences how we respond and maintain our relationships, ensuring that they are built on trust and transparency. Misunderstandings are a natural part of human communication, and they can typically be resolved through open and honest dialogue. When both parties are committed to understanding each other's perspectives and are willing to adjust their viewpoints, misunderstandings diminish and rarely leave lasting impacts on relationships.

On the other hand, manipulation involves a deliberate attempt by one party to influence or control another's thoughts or actions, often for personal gain. This can be seen in relationships where one person consistently denies or deflects from the truth to avoid accountability or to maintain an upper hand. For example, whenever a significant issue arises in a conversation, one person diverts the topic or falsely claims ignorance; this pattern might suggest manipulative intent rather than a simple misunderstanding. The key here is the persistence of such behaviors despite attempts to clarify or address the issues.

The intent behind words and actions plays a significant role in differentiating between manipulation and misunderstanding. Assessing intent involves observing whether there is a consistency between what a person says and what they do. Inconsistent messages often indicate manipulation. For instance, if someone professes care yet repeatedly acts in ways that contradict their stated feelings, this inconsistency can be a red flag. It is crucial to pay attention to these discrepancies as they often reveal underlying motives that are not aligned with the relationship's best interests.

Pattern recognition in communication aids immensely in identifying manipulative behaviors. Frequent inconsistencies, especially when coupled with justifications that aim to "explain away" discrepancies, indicate manipulation. Recognizing these patterns allows you to address potential manipulative tactics directly and assertively, helping to safeguard your emotional well-being and the integrity of your relationships.

Furthermore, seeking clarification is a powerful strategy in distinguishing manipulation from misunderstanding. Engaging in conversations that require direct answers can help reveal the truth behind someone's words. Asking open-ended questions that encourage detailed explanations can also prevent manipulative individuals from giving vague or evasive responses. For example, instead of asking, "Did you forget about our plans?" you might ask, "What happened that led to you missing our scheduled meeting?"

This type of questioning not only invites specificity but also reduces the wiggle room for manipulative responses, making it easier to gauge the honesty and intent of the other person.

In essence, understanding the subtle cues of communication and the consistency of actions over words is essential in navigating and maintaining healthy interpersonal relationships. Fostering an environment where open communication is encouraged and being vigilant about patterns that deviate from this norm can effectively differentiate between genuine misunderstandings and manipulation. This vigilance ensures that your relationships are built on a foundation of trust and mutual respect, where transparency is not just expected but actively practiced.

2.4 The Role of Denial in Gaslighting

One of the most insidious tools in the gaslighter's arsenal is denial. This tactic involves outright denying your experiences, effectively rejecting your perception of reality. Denial in gaslighting serves to confuse you and make you question the validity of your memories and emotions. It is a powerful technique because it targets your fundamental understanding of truth and can make you doubt even the most tangible experiences.

Imagine a scenario where, after a heated argument, you try to address the hurtful comments made by your partner. Instead of acknowledging the argument, your partner flatly denies it ever happened, asserting that you must have misunderstood or imagined the confrontation. This denial is not just frustrating—it is psychologically disorienting. It can make you question your memory or wonder if you are overreacting or misinterpreting the situation. Denial can also manifest in less direct ways, such as a partner minimizing events that you found traumatic or upsetting.

For instance, if you express hurt over a sarcastic remark they made, they might respond with something like, "I was just joking; you're too sensitive," thereby denying the validity of your feelings.

The impact of persistent denial on your emotional and psychological state can be profound. Regular exposure to denial can erode your trust in your own senses and judgments, leading to a diminished sense of self-trust. This erosion is not limited to interactions with the gaslighter but can extend to other areas of your life. You might find yourself hesitating to make decisions or second-guessing your perceptions in completely unrelated contexts, from work to social interactions. The long-term effects include increased anxiety, a pervasive sense of insecurity, and, in severe cases, a form of psychological paralysis where you are unable to act without external validation.

Counteracting denial requires a proactive approach. One effective strategy is to keep a detailed record of your interactions. This can be in the form of written notes, emails, text messages, or even audio recordings, where legally permissible. Documenting conversations and incidents provides you with a tangible reference that can affirm your reality and counteract attempts to rewrite or deny it. For example, if a conversation later gets denied or distorted, you can refer to your notes or the messages exchanged to confirm the facts. This practice not only helps in maintaining your grip on reality but also serves as a vital tool should you decide to seek help from a therapist or counselor, giving them a clear insight into the dynamics of your relationship.

Moreover, building a support network is crucial. Surround yourself with friends or family members who understand your situation and are willing to listen and validate your experiences without judgment. Sometimes, just hearing an outside perspective that aligns with your own can reinforce your confidence in your perceptions. Additionally, engaging with support groups, either online or in person, can connect you with others who have experienced similar situations. These communities can be invaluable in reaffirming that your experiences are real and do not result from misinterpretation or over-sensitivity.

Navigating out of the fog of gaslighting's denial is challenging yet essential for reclaiming your mental clarity and emotional health. By actively documenting interactions and fostering supportive relationships, you can protect your sense of reality and begin the process of healing from the psychological impacts of gaslighting. Remember, the goal is not just to counteract the gaslighter but to strengthen your trust in yourself, ensuring that your perceptions and feelings are validated and respected.

2.5 Responding to Gaslighting: First Steps

When you begin to feel the disorienting effects of gaslighting, the first and perhaps most crucial response is to trust that internal whisper that tells you something is not correct. Acknowledging to yourself that you are potentially being gaslighted is a significant step because it moves you from a place of confusion to one of proactive engagement. It is the initial shift from being a passive recipient of manipulation to an active seeker of clarity. Trusting your instincts is fundamental, as gaslighting primarily aims to make you doubt your perceptions, memories, and your sanity.

Reinforcing your personal reality is essential when facing gaslighting. One effective way to do this is through journaling. Keeping a daily log of your experiences and feelings helps maintain a personal record, which can be invaluable when your reality is being questioned. Write about events, conversations, and how they made you feel—this can help you keep track of the facts and your emotional responses, providing a baseline of reality that you can refer back to. Moreover, engaging in trusted conversations can be incredibly affirming. Speak with friends or family members who understand your situation and can provide external validation of your experiences. These conversations are not just comforting; they reaffirm your perceptions and strengthen your resolve against manipulative tactics.

Setting clear boundaries with someone who is gaslighting you is another crucial step. It involves directly communicating your understanding of reality and asserting that your perceptions are valid. Phrases like "I am confident in my memory of what happened" or "My feelings are valid and do not need justification" are ways to set boundaries assertively. These statements not only communicate your stance but also protect your mental space from further manipulation. It is essential to deliver these statements calmly and firmly, reinforcing your commitment to your truth without escalating the conflict.

Lastly, seeking support plays a pivotal role in dealing with the immediate effects of gaslighting and healing from its long-term impact. Professional help, such as therapy, can provide you with strategies to cope with the emotional turmoil and strengthen your psychological resilience. Therapists trained in dealing with emotional abuse can offer insights that go beyond your immediate network's support, providing tools that help untangle the complex feelings that gaslighting evokes. Additionally, support groups dedicated to those who have experienced similar forms of manipulation can offer comfort and advice, showing you that you are not alone in your experiences. These groups provide a community of understanding and support where you can learn from other's experiences and share your own, reinforcing the reality that your experiences are valid and that recovery is possible.

These steps form the foundation of responding to gaslighting. By acknowledging the issue, reinforcing your personal reality, setting clear boundaries, and seeking support, you equip yourself with the tools necessary to navigate out of the fog of manipulation. More importantly, these actions help you reclaim your autonomy and pave the way for healing, allowing you to engage in relationships with a renewed sense of confidence and clarity.

In summary, this chapter has guided you through the initial steps necessary to respond to gaslighting effectively. Beginning with the acknowledgment of the issue, it has covered the importance of trusting your perceptions, setting boundaries to safeguard your reality, and the critical role of seeking external support. These strategies are not just about countering manipulation but are also fundamental to restoring and maintaining your sense of self.

As we move forward, the next chapter builds on these foundations, exploring strategies to strengthen and heal your personal identity. This will involve delving deeper into understanding self-worth, enhancing resilience, and developing healthier relational dynamics. By continuing to build on the knowledge and strategies outlined so far, you will be better equipped to foster relationships that are supportive and nurturing, moving beyond survival to thriving in your interactions with others.

CHAPTER 3
THE IMPACT OF CODEPENDENCY

Have you ever felt like you are constantly pouring into others but seldom feel replenished yourself? This overwhelming sensation, often masked by a facade of selflessness, is a hallmark of something deeper and more complex—codependency. This chapter peels back the layers of codependency, exploring its roots, characteristics, and the psychological underpinnings that sustain it. By understanding codependency, you can start to unravel the threads that may be subtly woven into your relationships, allowing you to foster healthier connections.

3.1 What is Codependency? An In-depth Look

Codependency is often misunderstood as merely being overly reliant on relationships. However, it is more accurately described as a behavioral condition where one person enables another's addiction, poor mental health, immaturity, irresponsibility, or underachievement. This is an enabling behavior that typically stems from the caregiver's need to be needed, forming a cycle where the caregiver's identity and self-worth become contingent upon their role as a caretaker.

The term "codependency" originally surfaced in the context of addiction counseling, describing the enabling behaviors of family members toward an addicted individual. Over time, this term has broadened to encompass a more comprehensive array of relational dynamics where similar patterns of dependency, enabling, and control exist, regardless of the presence of an addiction. This evolution in understanding has allowed us to recognize codependency in romantic partnerships and across a spectrum of interpersonal relationships that can impact our lives.

Characteristically, codependent relationships are marked by an excess of caretaking. The codependent individual often puts the needs and well-being of others before their own, to the detriment of their personal health and happiness. This behavior is driven by an overwhelming need for approval and fear of rejection; thus, the codependent person often struggles with self-esteem issues. They may feel they must be needed to have any worth or that their value is derived solely from how much they can give to others.

From a psychological standpoint, theories such as attachment theory and family systems theory provide insight into why individuals may develop codependent traits. Attachment theory suggests that those with anxious or insecure attachments in childhood are more likely to seek out relationships that allow them to fulfill a caregiving or subservient role, as this may be their primary way of experiencing love and connection. Family systems theory further elucidates this by showing how families can operate as systems where roles are assigned that meet the emotional needs of the family rather than the individual. Children who grow up in such environments may learn to suppress their own needs to maintain family equilibrium, setting the stage for codependency in adult relationships.

Interactive Element: Reflective Journaling Exercise

To deepen your understanding of how codependency might be playing a role in your relationships, consider engaging in this reflective journaling exercise. Take a moment to write about a relationship in your life where you feel you might be giving more than you are receiving:

1. Describe how this relationship makes you feel on a daily basis.
2. Reflect on why you think you have taken on a caretaking role in this relationship.
3. Consider what fears or beliefs might be keeping you in this dynamic.
4. Imagine what this relationship might look like if it were more balanced.

This exercise is not just about awareness but also about beginning to consider what changes might be necessary for healthier relational dynamics.

By unpacking codependency through this in-depth exploration, we illuminate the patterns and behaviors that characterize it and set the stage for understanding its profound impact on individuals' lives and relationships. As we explore the signs and symptoms of codependency in the following sections, keep in mind this foundational knowledge, which will aid in recognizing and addressing these dynamics in your own life.

3.2 Signs You Might be in a Codependent Relationship

Recognizing the signs of codependency can often feel like trying to read a language you are only faintly familiar with. You sense something is off but cannot quite put your finger on what it is. Let us clarify some of these indicators to help you understand whether you are in a codependent relationship. A primary sign is experiencing difficulty in making independent decisions within the context of the relationship. This might manifest as hesitation or inability to choose simple things like what to eat or wear without seeking reassurance or approval from your partner. It often stems from a deep-seated fear of making mistakes that could upset the relational dynamics or displease your partner.

Another significant indicator is the need to control others' behavior, which paradoxically coexists with feelings of being controlled. You might find yourself excessively planning or managing circumstances to prevent adverse outcomes, which often relate to a partner's moods or actions. This could be as overt as dictating a partner's schedule or as subtle as emotionally manipulating situations to avoid potential conflict. This need for control is usually a response to an underlying anxiety about the relationship's stability. If you can keep everything in order, you can keep the relationship together and keep the peace.

Moreover, trouble identifying one's own feelings is a classic trait of codependency. When you are constantly attuned to another's emotional states and needs, you may start to disconnect from your own emotional responses. This can make you feel numb or confused about what you truly feel in different situations, making you dependent on your partner's emotional cues to dictate your own. For instance, if your partner is in a good mood, you feel happy and relieved; if they are upset, you might feel anxious or distressed, often disregarding the context of your own day. This codependency takes your focus off of your own feelings and inputs and validates only the others.

The emotional consequences of these signs are profound. Feelings of being trapped are common, where, despite being deeply unhappy or aware of the toxicity of the relationship, you might feel there is no way out without catastrophic consequences. This often links back to the fear of losing the relationship, which, despite its dysfunction, feels like a critical anchor. Excessive guilt for considering your needs or for times when you fail to 'keep the peace' can lead to anxiety, which perpetuates a cycle of self-neglect and over-focus on the other person. Chronic sadness or depression frequently emerges from the ongoing suppression of your own needs and identity, which, over time, dim the vibrancy of your life experience.

Behaviorally, these emotional states manifest in ways that are detrimental to both personal well-being and the health of the relationship. You might neglect your needs, skip meals, miss sleep, or forego social interactions to tend to someone else's needs. Staying in a clearly detrimental relationship, ignoring repeated red flags because you hold onto the hope that your sacrificial love will eventually change the dynamics, is a common yet painful manifestation of codependent behavior.

These behaviors and feelings significantly distort the balance and health of the relationship. What ideally should be a partnership becomes a caretaker-dependent dynamic, where one person's needs overshadow everything else, perpetuating the cycle of codependency. This imbalance impedes personal growth and satisfaction and creates a relationship environment where genuine intimacy and mutual support are replaced by neediness and resentment.

Understanding these signs and their implications can be disheartening, but it is a crucial step toward acknowledging the reality of the situation. Recognizing these patterns is the first move toward initiating change, both within oneself and in the dynamics of the relationship. As you reflect on these aspects, consider how they resonate with your experiences and what they might mean for your future steps. Remember, identifying the problem is the first step toward solving it.

3.3 Breaking Free from Codependency

Breaking free from codependency starts with the crucial step of recognizing and admitting the presence of codependent traits within oneself. This self-realization is not just a moment of insight; it is the opening of a door to a new way of interacting with the world, one that prioritizes your needs and emotional health. To embark on this path, begin by conducting an honest self-assessment. Take time to reflect on your relationships and identify patterns where your behavior might contribute to a codependent dynamic. Are there consistent instances where you find yourself sacrificing your happiness for the sake of another's needs? Do you often feel guilt when you prioritize yourself? Acknowledging these patterns can be challenging, as it involves confronting uncomfortable truths about how you relate to others. However, this acknowledgment is essential because it grounds your understanding of your role in sustaining these dynamics.

Once you have identified these traits, the next step is to foster autonomy within your relationships. Developing autonomy involves cultivating a sense of self that is independent of your relationships. Start by setting personal goals that are not tied to any other individual. These could be related to careers, personal hobbies, or educational pursuits. The key is focusing on aspirations that enhance your sense of identity and self-worth outside your usual caregiving role. For example, if you have always wanted to learn a new language or skill, pursuing this can shift your focus from others to yourself, reinforcing your sense of individuality.

Additionally, practicing decision-making in everyday situations can strengthen your confidence. Begin with small decisions, like choosing a restaurant or planning a day out, and gradually work up to more significant decisions. Each decision you make independently helps build a stronger sense of self, reducing the impulse to seek validation or direction from others.

Seeking professional help is another vital component in overcoming codependency. Therapy, particularly cognitive-behavioral therapy (CBT) and group therapy offers a structured environment where you can explore the roots of your codependent behaviors and develop strategies to alter them. CBT focuses on challenging and changing unhelpful cognitive distortions and behaviors, improving emotional regulation, and developing personal coping strategies that target solving current problems. It can be particularly effective in addressing the negative thought patterns that underpin codependency, such as fear of abandonment or feelings of unworthiness. Group therapy provides the added benefit of connecting with others who are facing similar challenges in their lives. Sharing your experiences in a supportive group setting can diminish feelings of isolation and provide diverse perspectives on handling codependent tendencies.

Creating and maintaining healthy boundaries is crucial in any attempt to break free from codependency. Boundaries are the guidelines we set for ourselves within relationships that dictate what we find acceptable and unacceptable. Establishing these boundaries involves clearly communicating your needs and limits with those around you. Start by identifying areas where your boundaries are being overlooked or violated in your relationships. Once these areas are clear, communicate your needs respectfully and clearly. For instance, if you need more time for yourself, you might say, "I value our time together, but I also need time to pursue my own interests. Let's find a balance that respects both our needs." It is important to be consistent in enforcing these boundaries; inconsistency can send mixed signals that may lead to boundaries being pushed or ignored.

As you implement these boundaries, remember that it is normal to experience resistance from those who are accustomed to your previous patterns of behavior. Stay firm and remind yourself why these boundaries are necessary for your well-being. Over time, consistently applying these strategies can shift the dynamics of your relationships toward healthier interactions where your needs are recognized and valued. This shift improves your personal happiness and models healthy relational patterns for those around you, encouraging them to reflect on and address their own behaviors.

Navigating the complexities of breaking free from codependency requires patience and compassion. You must remember that change does not happen overnight, and setbacks are a normal part of the journey towards healthier relationships. Each step you take, whether it is recognizing a codependent trait, setting a personal goal, seeking therapy, or establishing a boundary, is a move towards a more balanced and fulfilling life.

3.4 Building Individual Identity Beyond Relationships

Developing a solid sense of self that stands independent of your relationships is the cornerstone of a healthy, balanced life. This individual identity is your personal compass, guiding your decisions and interactions with the world around you. It is crucial, especially for those recovering from codependency, to cultivate an identity that is not defined by another person or by the role you play in someone else's life. Developing this sense of self involves engaging in activities and practices that foster personal growth and self-awareness.

One effective way to nurture your individual identity is through engaging in hobbies and educational pursuits that resonate with your personal interests. These activities allow you to explore aspects of your character and capabilities that are not tied to anyone else. For instance, taking up painting or writing can be incredibly liberating; these creative outlets offer a way to express your inner thoughts and emotions without external influence. Similarly, enrolling in courses that pique your interest or advance your career can boost your confidence and expand your horizons. Each step you take in these endeavors helps reinforce your sense of self-worth and independence.

Solo experiences, such as traveling alone or attending workshops and lectures, can also play a pivotal role in developing your self-identity. These experiences push you out of your comfort zone and challenge you to interact with the world independently. The decisions you make and the challenges you navigate while alone serve as powerful affirmations of your capabilities and strengths. Over time, these experiences build a robust sense of self that is not easily swayed by the opinions or needs of others. This newfound confidence is not just about knowing you can handle things on your own; it is about deeply understanding your preferences, dislikes, strengths, and limitations. Getting to know and understand the details of what makes you behave in a certain way will go toward understanding why you behave that way, too.

The role of self-reflection in this journey cannot be overstated. Practices like journaling and meditation offer valuable opportunities to converse with yourself, a dialogue that helps clarify your thoughts, feelings, and desires. Journaling, in particular, can be a cathartic experience where you pour your thoughts onto paper, sometimes uncovering hidden emotions or resolving internal conflicts. This practice can help track your growth over time, showing you how far you have come and where you might still want to go. Conversely, meditation allows you to sit with your thoughts quietly, which can be incredibly revealing. At first, this might be difficult, but It helps you develop an awareness of your mental and emotional patterns and provides a space to practice mindfulness. This skill enhances your ability to stay present and engaged in your own life rather than getting overly absorbed in the dynamics of others.

Learning to enjoy solitude is perhaps one of the most significant challenges for someone overcoming codependency. Solitude often carries a negative connotation, equated with loneliness. However, there is a profound difference between being lonely and enjoying solitude. Solitude is the state of being alone without being lonely, where you find joy and peace in your own company. Start small by setting aside short periods for solitude, perhaps spending these moments in nature or sitting quietly with a book. Gradually increase the time you spend alone, engaging in activities that you love, or simply sitting in reflection. Over time, solitude becomes a cherished space for rejuvenation and self-connection rather than a source of anxiety.

As you embark on these practices, remember that building an individual identity is a dynamic, ongoing process. It does not happen overnight, nor is it something that, once achieved, remains static. Your sense of self will evolve as you grow and change, influenced by your experiences, aspirations, and the relationships you choose to nurture along the way. By investing in this personal growth, you not only enhance your own life but also enrich the way you interact with others, bringing to your relationships a whole, fulfilled individual. This transformation allows for healthier interactions and more balanced dynamics with those around you, fostering connections based on mutual respect and genuine affection that will withstand time and not be fleeting.

3.5 Codependency Across Different Types of Relationships

The tendrils of codependency are not confined to the romantic sphere; they can weave their way into any relationship dynamic where a disproportionate reliance exists on others for emotional support or validation. This can occur in familial setups, friendships, and even professional environments, each presenting unique challenges and manifestations. Understanding how codependency molds these different relationships can illuminate paths to healthier interactions across all areas of your life.

In family relationships, codependency often finds its roots in the established roles each member plays within the unit. For instance, a parent might become codependent on a child, relying on the child for emotional support and decision-making, which blurs the boundaries of parental responsibility and child independence. Conversely, a child might feel responsible for the emotional well-being of a parent, often stepping into a caretaker role prematurely. This dynamic can stunt the child's emotional and social development as they prioritize the parent's needs over their own growth and exploration of the world.

Friendships can also succumb to codependent patterns, particularly when one friend consistently acts as the 'helper' or 'rescuer,' deriving their sense of worth from their ability to solve or alleviate the problems of the other. While it might appear noble or generous, over time, this imbalance can breed resentment and emotional exhaustion in the caretaker, as well as dependency and lack of initiative in the receiver. Such friendships might struggle with establishing a give-and-take balance, instead revolving around crises and the constant need for support, which can overshadow the joy and reciprocity that true friendship should bring.

Professional relationships are not immune to codependency either. In the workplace, you might find yourself overextending to meet the demands or expectations of colleagues or superiors, often at the expense of your well-being and professional boundaries. This can be particularly challenging to navigate, as the lines between supporting team goals and jeopardizing one's health can often become blurred in high-stress environments or in cultures that prize overachievement in the workplace.

Addressing codependency in these varied relationships requires tailored strategies that respect the unique dynamics and roles involved. In family relationships, it is crucial to redefine roles that support individual growth and autonomy. This might include setting boundaries around responsibilities or seeking family therapy to address and recalibrate unhealthy dependencies developed over the years. Friendships are about fostering mutuality, encouraging both parties to contribute to the relationship's health by sharing responsibilities, supporting each other, and celebrating individual achievements without one overshadowing the other.

In professional settings, overcoming codependency might be asserting your boundaries more clearly, such as defining work hours or seeking roles and responsibilities that allow you to thrive independently without constant oversight or approval from others. It is also beneficial to cultivate a support network outside of work to ensure that your self-esteem and emotional validation are not solely dependent on your professional success or recognition.

A healthy alternative to these codependent dynamics is fostering relationships based on healthy interdependence. Interdependent relationships are characterized by mutual support that does not compromise individual strength and autonomy. Each person in an interdependent relationship feels free to pursue their interests and obligations, knowing that their relationships are not contingent on sacrificing these pursuits. Instead, there is a supportive framework that celebrates individual achievements and collaboratively solves challenges without over-reliance on one party.

By recognizing and adjusting the patterns of codependency in various types of relationships, you can cultivate a life rich in healthy, supportive interactions that empower rather than limit you. The sky is the limit in your relationships with others. This shift enhances your personal well-being and sets a foundation for current and future relationships to thrive on mutual respect and genuine connectivity.

As we conclude this chapter, remember that codependency does not define you or your capacity to forge meaningful connections. It is merely a pattern—one that you have the power to transform. With the insights and strategies discussed, you are equipped to nurture healthier relationships across all facets of your life, ensuring that your interactions are as fulfilling as they are supportive.

The next chapter will delve into practical tools and strategies to solidify these healthier relational dynamics, ensuring you have the resources to maintain the balance between caring for others and nurturing yourself. This balance is important for sustained emotional health and relationship satisfaction, providing a stable foundation for all your personal and professional interactions.

CHAPTER 4

SELF-WORTH AND SELF-PERCEPTION

Have you ever paused in front of a mirror, not just to check your appearance, but to really look at yourself and wonder, "What do I value in the person staring back at me?" This chapter is about those moments of reflection—about understanding, assessing, and ultimately nurturing your sense of self-worth. It is about stripping away layers of external influence to discover the genuine value you hold within yourself, not as defined by others but as cherished by you.

4.1 Assessing Self-Worth: A Self-Reflective Journey

Embarking on the journey of self-worth assessment is akin to setting out on a path of self-discovery with a map that only you can complete. It is about marking the landmarks of your inner strengths and values and, sometimes, revisiting the shadows where negative perceptions might lurk. To begin this exploration, it is essential to introduce tools and methods that facilitate this introspection. Reflective journaling stands out as a profoundly effective technique, serving as both a mirror and a map, reflecting your current self-image while guiding you toward a deeper understanding of your intrinsic value. Similarly, structured questionnaires focused on self-perception can provide a framework for this assessment, helping you systematically explore and evaluate your self-worth.

Identifying the sources of your self-worth involves a careful examination of what currently defines your sense of value. For many, self-worth is significantly shaped by external validations—praise from peers, achievements in the workplace, or even the number of likes on a social media post. While these sources can provide temporary boosts, they often lead to a fragile sense of self-worth that fluctuates with external circumstances. Instead, this chapter encourages you to discover and cultivate internal sources of self-worth, such as resilience, compassion, or creativity. These intrinsic qualities offer a more stable foundation for self-esteem because they are not dependent on external recognition.

Reflecting on how past relationships and upbringing have influenced your self-worth is another critical step in this journey. Our interactions with family, friends, and partners can profoundly impact how we view ourselves. Reflective questions such as, "How did the significant people in my life speak about my abilities and worth?" or "What messages did I receive about my value from these relationships?" can help uncover the roots of your current self-perception. These reflections reveal both positive influences that you might want to embrace and negative impressions that may require reevaluation and healing.

The path toward enhancing your self-worth begins with these gentle yet powerful initial steps. Transitioning from a negative self-assessment to a more positive self-view requires patience and self-compassion. This process is not about overhauling your person-

ality overnight but about making incremental changes that reinforce your intrinsic worth and will significantly impact your
perception of yourself. It involves recognizing and challenging
long-held beliefs about yourself, affirming your strengths, and
forgiving yourself for past self-judgments. This gradual shift
fosters a healthier self-image and enhances your overall well-
being.

Interactive Element: Self-Worth Assessment Exercise

To concretely apply the insights from this section, consider
engaging in the following reflective exercise:

1. **Journal Prompt:** Write about three qualities you
   genuinely appreciate about yourself that do not depend
   on anyone else's approval.
2. **Questionnaire:** Complete a self-worth assessment that
   rates aspects such as independence, ability to handle
   criticism, and openness to self-improvement.
3. **Reflection:** After completing the questionnaire, reflect on
   any surprises or insights you discovered. What areas of
   your self-worth would you like to strengthen?

By integrating these reflective practices into your routine, you
begin to lay down the stepping stones on your path toward a
richer, more self-affirmed life. Each step and discovery adds a
layer of understanding and appreciation for the unique individual
you are beyond the shadows of doubt and the echoes of past validations. This chapter not only guides you through the process of
assessing and understanding your self-worth but also lights the
way for the journey ahead, where each step is a progression
towards embracing and enhancing your true self.

4.2 Practices to Rebuild and Enhance Self-Esteem

Building self-esteem is akin to nurturing a garden; it requires regular attention, care, and sometimes landscape restructuring. One of the foundational practices in cultivating healthy self-esteem is using positive affirmations. When spoken repeatedly, these are short, powerful statements that can help to reprogram the subconscious mind, encouraging a shift from negative thought patterns to a more positive outlook on oneself and life. For example, starting your day by affirming, "I am worthy of respect and love," or "I possess the skills to handle whatever comes my way," can significantly impact how you feel about yourself throughout the day. These affirmations reinforce your values and capabilities, which, in turn, boost your self-esteem.

Incorporating self-care routines is another vital practice. Self-care goes beyond the occasional spa day; it encompasses any activity that you do deliberately to take care of your mental, emotional, and physical health. This could be as simple as setting aside time each night to read, taking a walk in nature, or engaging in a hobby that you love. Regular self-care reminds you that you are worth the time and effort, which is fundamental to building self-esteem. Moreover, setting small, achievable goals can also play a crucial role. These goals give you something concrete to work towards, and each accomplishment can boost your confidence, no matter how small. It could be as simple as committing to a 10-minute meditation each morning or completing a small project. The key is consistency and achievable targets, which together build a foundation of success that bolsters your self-esteem.

The role of physical health in influencing self-esteem is profound. Regular physical activity, such as yoga, jogging, or even dancing, improves your physical well-being and significantly impacts your mental health. Exercise releases endorphins, known as 'feel-good' hormones, which can enhance your mood and outlook on life. A healthy diet also plays a critical role. Nutritious foods nourish the body and brain, affecting your energy levels and cognitive functions and influencing how you feel about yourself. Nutrient-dense foods will nourish your body and give you more energy. Encouraging the integration of physical wellness into your daily routine can be a powerful tool in building a more positive self-image and improving overall mental health.

Social interactions also play a crucial role in shaping self-esteem. The people you choose to surround yourself with can either uplift or drain you. Engaging with supportive, positive people can reinforce your self-worth through positive feedback and encouragement. Conversely, relationships that consistently leave you feeling undervalued or disrespected can have a detrimental impact on your self-esteem. It is essential to be mindful of the company you keep, choosing to spend time with those who respect you and reflect the values you aspire to embody. This might mean setting boundaries or even distancing yourself from those who consistently undermine your self-worth. By actively choosing healthier relationships, you create a social environment that supports and enhances your self-esteem.

Lifelong learning and self-improvement are also vital in enhancing self-esteem. The pursuit of knowledge and new skills not only enriches your life but also bolsters your self-confidence. Whether learning a new language, picking up a new skill, or delving into a field of study that fascinates you, each new learning experience adds to your sense of competence and achievement. These pursuits challenge you, pushing you out of your comfort zone and enabling personal growth, which is intrinsically linked to self-esteem. They remind you of your potential to evolve and adapt, qualities that are essential to a resilient self-image.

Integrating these practices into your daily life sets the stage for a robust and resilient self-esteem that can withstand the challenges life throws your way. Each step, whether repeating an empowering affirmation, making time for a jog, engaging in meaningful social interactions, or learning something new, builds upon the last, creating a composite of a well-nurtured and confident self.

4.3 Overcoming Internalized Negative Messages

One of the most significant barriers to achieving a healthy self-perception is the presence of internalized negative messages. These messages, often echo past criticisms or the residue of toxic relationships, can persistently whisper in your mind, shaping how you view yourself and your abilities. Identifying these messages is the first step in transforming them. It involves listening to the dialogue that runs through your mind and noting the times when you are being particularly critical of yourself. Are these thoughts factual, or are they distortions of your reality? More often than not, they are the latter. Strategies to challenge these negative beliefs include questioning their validity, tracing their origins, and consciously replacing them with positive affirmations that reinforce your true worth.

Therapeutic techniques, especially Cognitive Behavioral Therapy (CBT), offer a structured approach to altering these detrimental thought patterns. CBT focuses on understanding the connections between thoughts, emotions, and behaviors and employs strategies to modify these thoughts to improve emotional regulation and develop personal coping strategies. For example, if you frequently find yourself believing that you are unworthy of success, CBT techniques would encourage you to challenge this belief with evidence of your past accomplishments and capabilities, thereby reshaping your thought patterns to be more supportive and less critical. Engaging in CBT with a skilled therapist can provide you with the tools to combat negative self-talk and foster a more compassionate dialogue with yourself.

Forgiveness, particularly self-forgiveness, is a powerful tool in healing and overcoming the impact of negative messages. Holding onto past mistakes or harboring guilt can keep you trapped in a cycle of negative self-worth. Learning to forgive yourself and accept that you did the best you could at the moment with the knowledge and resources you had are crucial in moving forward. This forgiveness also extends to others who may have contributed to these negative messages. Letting go of resentment can liberate a significant amount of emotional energy, which can then be redirected toward building a more positive self-image and a fulfilling life.

Maintaining a positive environment plays a crucial role in reinforcing new, positive messages about yourself. This involves curating your media consumption to ensure that the content you engage with supports your sense of self-worth and reflects your values. Similarly, hobbies that resonate with your soul and provide a sense of accomplishment can reinforce your confidence and enhance your life satisfaction. Moreover, the company you keep can profoundly impact how you feel about yourself. Surrounding yourself with supportive, uplifting people can provide an external buffer against negative self-talk and enhance your emotional resilience. These elements collectively create a nurturing environment that supports your journey towards a healthier self-perception, allowing you to thrive despite the challenges you may face. This positive environment acts as a sanctuary and a garden where your newly formed self-esteem can flourish, supported by the pillars of forgiveness, therapeutic growth, and continuous personal validation.

4.4 Setting Realistic Self-Expectations

When we talk about setting goals, there is often an unspoken pressure to aim for the stars—to set ambitious targets that, while inspiring, might stretch beyond our current capacities. It is crucial, however, to cultivate a balance between ambition and realism in your goal-setting practices. This balance prevents the discouragement that comes from setting and failing to achieve unrealistically high expectations. For instance, if you are new to exercise, setting a goal to run a marathon in a month is unrealistic and potentially harmful. Instead, a more achievable goal would be to start with shorter, more frequent walks, gradually building up your stamina. This approach sets you up for success and reinforces your confidence as you meet each incremental goal.

Understanding and respecting your personal limits plays a significant role in sustainable self-growth. Each person has unique capacities and limits, which can vary depending on many factors, including physical health, emotional state, and external pressures. Listening to your body and mind and recognizing signs of strain or stress is essential, which might indicate that your current pace or expectations are too demanding. Respecting these limits is not about capping your potential but about growing at a pace that maintains your health and well-being, ensuring that your pursuits are constructive rather than destructive.

In the realm of relationships, setting realistic expectations is equally important. It is essential to seek out and nurture relationships that respect your boundaries and contribute positively to your sense of self-worth. For example, if continuous emotional support from a partner is important to you, expecting them to provide this is reasonable. However, expecting a partner to solve all your personal issues is not only unrealistic but may also lead to dependency and disappointment. Instead, aim for a balance where both partners support each other without overstepping personal boundaries or relying solely on each other for emotional fulfillment. This balance helps ensure that relationships enhance your life rather than creating additional stress or diminishing your self-esteem.

Dealing with setbacks is an inevitable part of life. No matter how well you plan or how hard you work, there will be times when things go differently than expected. It is vital to view these moments not as failures but as opportunities for learning and growth. For instance, if a job interview does not lead to an offer, try to extract lessons from the experience instead of dwelling on the disappointment. Could your interview skills be improved? Did you fully understand the job requirements? Addressing these questions can turn a setback into a stepping stone towards future success. Additionally, trying to maintain a resilient mindset helps in coping with setbacks. Resilience can be fostered by staying committed to your goals, adapting your strategies as needed, and remaining connected with supportive individuals who encourage your growth.

By adopting these strategies—balancing ambition with realism, understanding your limits, setting appropriate expectations in relationships, and learning from setbacks—you develop a more grounded and resilient approach to personal and professional growth. This approach enhances your ability to achieve your goals and supports a healthier, more satisfying life. As you continue to navigate your path, remember that each step taken with awareness and adaptability is a step towards a more fulfilled and self-aware existence.

4.5 Celebrating Self-Progress and Small Wins

Recognizing and celebrating every small victory along your path to greater self-worth is beneficial and essential. It is easy to overlook the small steps forward or to dismiss them as insignificant in the grand scheme of things. However, these moments are the foundation of sustainable self-growth and deserve acknowledgment. Each time you recognize your progress, no matter how minor it may seem, you reinforce your commitment to personal growth and boost your motivation to continue. This practice turns the journey into a series of victories, not just a distant goal to be reached.

The concept of a 'victory log' can be particularly transformative in this process. This personal record acts as a tangible reminder of your successes, allowing you to see the accumulation of your efforts over time. You can start by jotting down daily or weekly achievements in a notebook or digital document. These entries can be as simple as, "Today, I spoke up about my ideas during a meeting," or "This week, I managed to set aside time for my personal hobby." The act of writing down these victories helps solidify them in your mind, making them more real and giving you a concrete reason to celebrate your growth.

Sharing these successes with supportive friends, family, or members of a supportive group can amplify their impact. When you vocalize your achievements and receive positive reinforcement from others, it boosts your morale and strengthens your social connections. These moments of sharing can become pillars of encouragement in your journey, reminding you that you are not alone and that your efforts are recognized and appreciated by others. Furthermore, by sharing your progress, you contribute to a culture of positivity and motivation for yourself and those around you.

Integrating celebration into your daily life can also enhance your overall well-being. Establishing small rituals or habits that acknowledge your growth can make a significant difference. For example, you might treat yourself to a favorite coffee or a special meal every time you meet a small goal, or you could set aside a few moments each evening to reflect on and savor the day's successes. These rituals do not have to be elaborate; their real value lies in their regularity and the personal meaning they hold. Making the celebration a regular part of your life creates a positive feedback loop that perpetuates further growth and happiness.

Embracing this celebratory approach to personal development fosters a mindset that recognizes and values growth in all its forms. It shifts your focus from what is left to achieve to what has been achieved, filling your journey with gratitude and positive energy. This shift makes the process more enjoyable and sustainable, as it builds an enduring foundation of self-appreciation and confidence.

As this chapter closes, remember that each step forward, no matter how small, is a step toward becoming the person you aspire to be. Celebrating these steps is not just about giving yourself a pat on the back—it is about building a ladder of achievements that elevates your sense of self-worth and propels you forward. You are building a mosaic of accomplishments, each piece important and worth celebrating, culminating in a vibrant portrayal of your growth and resilience.

In the next chapter, we will explore the dynamics of establishing and maintaining boundaries—a critical component of fostering respectful and supportive relationships that reflect and enhance your growing sense of self-worth. Here, you will learn how to assertively communicate your needs and expectations, ensuring that your relationships contribute positively to your life just as you enrich the lives of others. This continuation is not just about protecting yourself; it is about creating interactions that respect and celebrate the individual you are becoming.

CHAPTER 5
ESTABLISHING AND
ENFORCING BOUNDARIES

Have you ever felt as if you were giving too much of yourself away, leaving little behind for your own well-being? This feeling may signal a need to examine and redefine your relationships' boundaries. Boundaries are the guidelines we set for ourselves and others; they help define our sense of self and are vital for maintaining a healthy relationship balance. They are not walls meant to shut people out but rather personal parameters that ensure mutual respect and understanding.

5.1 The Importance of Boundaries in Healthy Relationships

Boundaries serve as personal property lines that mark our responsibilities. In relationships, boundaries help us define ourselves in relation to others. They indicate what we are comfortable with and how we expect to be treated by others. Healthy boundaries can prevent relationships from becoming overwhelming and consuming, thereby preserving our individuality.

In romantic relationships, a healthy boundary might be having regular time apart to pursue individual interests, which can enhance personal growth and bring fresh energy into the relationship. Conversely, an example of an unhealthy boundary in a romantic setting might be one partner demanding access to the other's personal communications, like texts and emails, which infringes on privacy and trust.

In family relationships, healthy boundaries might involve limiting one another's expectations and ensuring that each family member feels respected and not taken for granted. An unhealthy boundary in a familial context could be a parent relying on a child to fulfill their emotional needs, which can burden the child with inappropriate responsibilities and hinder their development.

Professionally, setting boundaries can ensure that work demands do not encroach excessively on personal time. An example of a healthy boundary at work would be not answering work emails during family dinners. On the other hand, a lack of boundaries in the workplace might manifest as accepting tasks well beyond your job role or working longer hours, leading to burnout and resentment.

These boundaries are not just about saying no but about opening the door to honest and respectful communication about your needs and limits. They help safeguard your emotional well-being and ensure that your relationships are mutually supportive and fulfilling. By clearly defining what is acceptable and what is not, boundaries help prevent misunderstandings and conflicts, making each relationship more enjoyable and healthier.

Another significant aspect of setting boundaries is the prevention of burnout and resentment. Without clear boundaries, you may find yourself overextended, feeling like you are giving too much in your relationships, whether they are personal or professional. This overextension can lead to exhaustion and feeling unappreciated, which are common precursors to resentment. By setting and enforcing boundaries, you ensure that you engage in relationships in a way that sustains your energy and enthusiasm in life and toward your relationships.

Visual Element: Reflective Exercise - Boundary Mapping

To better understand and visualize your current boundaries, try this reflective exercise:

1. Draw a circle on a piece of paper and write your name in the middle.
2. Think about the different types of relationships in your life (romantic, family, friends, professional) and draw them around your central circle as smaller circles.
3. For each relationship, draw the circle closer or further from your central circle based on how much energy you feel the relationship takes from you.
4. Reflect on each relationship:

- Is the proximity of the circle appropriate based on how much you want to give to this relationship?
- Are there relationships that are too close, perhaps indicating weak boundaries?
- Are there relationships that are too distant, possibly showing too rigid boundaries?

This exercise can help you visualize which relationships might need healthier boundaries. It acts as a starting point for considering where adjustments are necessary to maintain your emotional health and relationship satisfaction.

By understanding and adjusting your boundaries, you protect your well-being and also cultivate deeper and more meaningful connections with those around you. Boundaries allow you to respect yourself and others, fostering care and respect in all interactions, which are fundamental to any healthy relationship dynamic.

5.2 Steps to Establishing Firm Boundaries

Establishing firm boundaries in your relationships involves a delicate balance of self-reflection, clear communication, and consistent enforcement. The first step in this process is self-reflection to identify your own needs and limits. This reflective practice lets you understand what makes you uncomfortable or stressed and why. It is about tuning into your feelings and recognizing situations or behaviors that cause discomfort. For instance, you might feel drained after spending too much time with a particular friend, or you might feel stressed when work calls encroach on your personal time. Understanding these feelings when they occur helps you pinpoint where boundaries must be set.

Once you have identified these needs, the next crucial step is clearly and assertively communicating these boundaries to others. Effective communication of your boundaries involves expressing your needs directly and respectfully without being aggressive or apologetic. It is essential to use clear, straightforward language that leaves no room for misunderstanding. For example, suppose you decide you cannot accept work calls during family dinners. In that case, a straightforward way to communicate this might be, "I value our project, and I want to give it my full attention, which is why I will not be taking work calls during family dinners. I'll be available again after 7 PM." This statement is direct and respectful, setting a clear boundary without aggression or guilt.

Navigating these conversations, especially when they concern changing longstanding dynamics, requires tact and careful consideration. One practical tip is to choose the right time and place to have these conversations. This means selecting a moment when both parties are relaxed and can give the discussion their full attention, rather than in the heat of a conflict or during a stressful period. Additionally, using "I" statements can help to keep the discussion from becoming accusatory. For example, saying, "I feel overwhelmed when I have to answer emails on weekends," centers the conversation around your feelings and needs rather than what the other person is doing wrong. Staying calm throughout the entire discussion also helps to keep the conversation constructive, preventing escalation and fostering mutual understanding.

Finally, the reinforcement of these boundaries through consistency is what ensures their respect and longevity in the relationship. Inconsistency in boundary-setting can lead to confusion and can undermine your efforts, making it seem like the boundaries are negotiable. This can cause confusion or lead to the boundaries being tested more often. It is essential to stick to the boundaries you've set, even when it's challenging. Consistency sends a clear message that you are serious about your needs and that these boundaries are essential for your well-being. Over time, as these boundaries are consistently respected, they will become a natural part of your interactions, contributing to healthier and more balanced relationships.

By integrating self-reflection, clear communication, practical tips for difficult conversations, and consistency in enforcement, you create a robust framework for establishing and maintaining boundaries that protect your well-being and enhance your relationships. This approach supports your personal growth and fosters a climate of respect and care in your interactions, making each relationship more fulfilling and aligned with your needs, which can enrich your life and the lives of others.

5.3 Dealing with Boundary Pushback

When you decide to set and enforce new boundaries, it is natural to encounter some resistance. People who are used to old dynamics might react in various ways, from mild discomfort to outright anger or manipulation. Anticipating these reactions helps you prepare mentally and emotionally, ensuring you can maintain your boundaries without escalating tensions.

Firstly, it is common for people to test boundaries, not always out of disrespect, but sometimes simply to understand the limits. This testing can manifest as repeated requests or pushing back against your boundaries to see if you truly stand by them. Anger or frustration might also surface, especially if the new boundaries significantly affect someone else's behavior or habits. For instance, if you decide not to lend money to a friend as you have done routinely, this friend might react negatively at first, perceiving your boundary as a withdrawal of friendship or support.

Maintaining your stance calmly and assertively is crucial to handle these reactions effectively. It involves clear, consistent communication and the confidence to reiterate your boundaries without aggression. If a situation begins to escalate, de-escalation tactics become essential. Techniques such as keeping your tone even, not over-explaining your reasons, and, if necessary, removing yourself from a heated situation can help manage and mitigate conflict. Sometimes, simply stating, "I understand this is upsetting, but I need to stick to what's best for me," can reaffirm your boundary while acknowledging the other person's feelings. Change takes time sometimes, and consistency is essential.

Feelings of guilt and the manipulation tactics of others can be particularly challenging to navigate. You might feel guilty for saying no or for causing others discomfort, especially if those individuals express hurt or disappointment. It is important to remind yourself that setting boundaries is not just about saying no to others but saying yes to a healthier, more balanced life for yourself. Manipulation can often play on these feelings of guilt with statements like, "If you really cared, you wouldn't do this." In these instances, it is vital to recognize manipulation for what it is—a tactic to coerce you into giving up your boundaries. Staying firm in these situations means gently but firmly reiterating your boundary, reminding yourself and the other person why this boundary is necessary for your well-being.

Seeking support plays a significant role when you face strong resistance or manipulation. Turning to trusted friends, family, or professionals can provide you with a reinforcement of your decision to set boundaries. These supports can offer emotional comfort and practical advice on handling pushback. They serve as a sounding board, giving you a perspective outside the immediate emotional responses. This can be crucial in maintaining your resolve and ensuring you do not feel isolated in your efforts to change dynamics that no longer serve you well.

In setting boundaries, you are effectively advocating for your values and your right to emotional and mental well-being. While pushback can be an uncomfortable hurdle, navigating it with calmness, consistency, and support can reinforce your boundaries and gradually lead others to respect them. This process strengthens your relationships and deepens your self-respect as you honor your needs and limits. By firmly and compassionately standing by your boundaries, you teach others how to treat you and what you are willing to accept, shaping the dynamics around you in more healthy and respectful ways.

5.4 Maintaining Boundaries in High-Pressure Situations

Navigating high-pressure situations while maintaining your boundaries can often feel like walking a tightrope. These scenarios, whether they are charged family dinners, critical business meetings, or heated discussions with a partner, test the resilience of the boundaries you have set for yourself. Identifying these situations beforehand allows you to prepare mentally and emotionally, ensuring that you can uphold your limits even under stress. For example, family gatherings might bring up old dynamics that challenge your newly established boundaries. In professional settings, high-stakes meetings may pressure you to conform to group opinions, sidelining your own perspectives. And in personal relationships, emotionally charged arguments can tempt you to compromise your boundaries just to reach a quick resolution.

To navigate these situations effectively, having a strategy in place is crucial. One practical approach is to develop exit strategies beforehand. For instance, if a family gathering becomes too overwhelming, you might plan to take a brief walk to gather your thoughts and emotions. In a professional context, if a meeting begins to infringe on your boundaries, having a polite, prepared statement can help you excuse yourself or redirect the conversation. These exit strategies provide a physical break from the tension and give you a moment to reaffirm your commitment to your boundaries.

Utilizing calming techniques before and during these situations can also play a significant role in maintaining your composure and boundaries. Techniques such as deep breathing, mindfulness, or even a brief guided meditation session can center your thoughts and reduce the emotional intensity, equipping you to handle potential boundary challenges more effectively. For instance, before entering a challenging meeting or family event, take a few minutes to practice deep breathing exercises, which can help lower your stress levels and enhance your focus.

Role-playing scenarios are another invaluable tool for preparing to maintain boundaries under pressure. Engaging in role-play with a therapist or a trusted friend can help you anticipate potential conflicts and rehearse your responses. This preparation can increase your confidence and ability to assert your boundaries during actual high-pressure situations. For example, you might role-play a scenario where a family member questions your career choices and practice responding in a way that respects your decisions and maintains your boundaries.

After facing a high-pressure situation, regardless of the outcome, engaging in self-care is vital. It is up to you to take time to replenish yourself. High-stress interactions can be draining, making it essential to take time to recover and reaffirm your sense of self-worth. Activities that restore your peace and reinforce your boundaries are key. This might involve activities like journaling, where you can process your feelings and evaluate how well you maintained your boundaries. Alternatively, engaging in a favorite hobby or spending time in nature can help restore your energy and reduce stress. These acts of self-care are vital, not just for recovery, but for building resilience against future boundary challenges.

By recognizing potential high-pressure situations, preparing with strategies like exit plans and calming techniques, practicing through role-playing, and prioritizing post-confrontation self-care, you empower yourself to uphold your boundaries even under the most challenging circumstances. This approach protects your emotional and mental well-being and consistently strengthens your ability to advocate for yourself across all areas of life.

5.5 Boundaries and Self-Respect

When you set boundaries, you are not just protecting your time, energy, and emotional well-being; you are also engaging in an act of self-respect. This declaration of your worth teaches others how to treat you and sets a standard for what you expect and accept in your relationships. Imagine a scenario where you consistently make your needs and limits clear; this reinforces your self-respect and models how others should interact with you, fostering reciprocal respect. It is like setting the rules of a game before playing— it ensures everyone knows what is expected and how to behave, leading to a smoother, more respectful interaction.

Maintaining firm boundaries has a profoundly positive impact on your self-image and confidence. Each time you uphold your boundaries, you affirm to yourself that your needs are important. This reinforcement builds your self-worth as you recognize and act upon your right to be treated well. It is akin to building a muscle; the more you exercise it, the stronger it becomes. In the context of self-image, each act of maintaining boundaries builds your confidence muscle, making you feel more empowered and assertive. Over time, this does not just affect how you see yourself; it also influences how others perceive you. They see a person who values themselves and is not afraid to stand up for their well-being, which can lead to greater respect and less likelihood of boundary violations.

Furthermore, setting and respecting your own boundaries can serve as a powerful model for others, potentially transforming the dynamics of your social circle. When friends and family see you implementing and maintaining healthy boundaries, it can inspire them to examine and assert their own limits. This modeling can create a ripple effect, improving the overall health of your community's interpersonal dynamics. For example, you consistently leave work at a reasonable hour to prioritize family time. In that case, your colleagues might feel empowered to do the same, gradually shifting the work culture towards more sustainable work-life balance practices.

Boundaries are essential for mutual respect in any relationship. They provide clear guidelines for how individuals can interact in ways that respect each other's personal space, feelings, and needs. Without boundaries, relationships can quickly become unbalanced, leading to feelings of resentment and misunderstanding. By setting boundaries, you invite others to interact with you in a respectful and considerate manner, promoting healthier and more balanced relationships. This mutual respect enhances individual relationships and fosters a general atmosphere of understanding and consideration that can extend beyond personal interactions to influence our broader social interactions.

In setting boundaries, you essentially communicate your value to those around you. You teach them that your emotions, time, and opinions are worthy of respect. This, in turn, encourages them to recognize and respect their worth, fostering a cycle of positive self-regard and respect among all parties involved. This cycle can significantly enhance the quality of your interactions, making your social circle a more supportive and enriching environment.

By embracing the practice of setting and maintaining boundaries, you advocate for your well-being and empower those around you to do the same. This empowerment leads to more meaningful and satisfying relationships characterized by mutual respect and understanding. As you continue to grow in your boundary-setting skills, remember that each step you take benefits you and contributes to the well-being of your relationships and the broader community.

As we wrap up this chapter on boundaries, we have explored the profound impact that setting and maintaining boundaries has on our self-respect, self-image, and the dynamics of our relationships. We have learned that these practices enhance our lives and serve as a model for others, promoting a culture of respect and mutual understanding. As we move forward, we must remember that boundaries are not barriers but bridges to healthier, more respectful, and fulfilling interactions.

The next chapter will delve into the complexities of recognizing and responding to red flags in relationships. This knowledge is crucial for navigating away from potentially harmful situations and toward safer, more rewarding interactions with individuals. By learning to identify and act upon these warning signs, you can protect yourself and cultivate relationships that genuinely add value to your life.

MAKE A DIFFERENCE WITH YOUR REVIEW

UNLOCK THE POWER OF GENEROSITY

"The best way to find yourself is to lose yourself in the service of others."

— MAHATMA GANDHI

People who give without expectation live longer, happier lives and make a bigger impact. So, if we've got a chance to do that together, I'm going to give it my all.

To make that happen, I have a question for you...

Would you help someone you've never met, even if you never got credit for it?

Who is this person you ask? They are like you. Or, at least, like you used to be. Feeling trapped in a toxic relationship, wanting to make a change, and needing guidance but not sure where to turn.

Our mission is to make freedom from toxic relationships accessible to everyone. Everything I do stems from that mission. And the only way for me to accomplish that mission is by reaching... well...everyone.

This is where you come in. Most people do, in fact, judge a book by its cover (and its reviews). So here's my ask on behalf of a struggling reader you've never met:

Please help that reader by leaving this book a review.

Your gift costs no money and less than 60 seconds to make real, but can change a fellow reader's life forever. Your review could help...

- ...one more person break free from emotional manipulation.
- ...one more individual regain their self-worth.
- ...one more soul find the courage to leave a toxic relationship.
- ...one more person discover the joy of healthy, supportive relationships.
- ...one more dream of a happy, fulfilling life come true.

To get that 'feel good' feeling and help this person for real, all you have to do is...and it takes less than 60 seconds... leave a review.

Simply scan the QR code to leave your review:

If you feel good about helping a faceless reader, you are my kind of person. Welcome to the club. You're one of us.

I'm that much more excited to help you achieve freedom from toxic relationships faster and more completely than you can possibly imagine. You'll love the insights and strategies I'm about to share in the coming chapters.

Thank you from the bottom of my heart. Now, back to our regularly scheduled program.

- Your biggest fan, Piper Madison

PS - Fun fact: If you provide something of value to another person, it makes you more valuable to them. If you believe this book will help someone you know, please share it with them.

CHAPTER 6

RECOGNIZING AND RESPONDING TO RED FLAGS

Have you ever felt that unsettling twinge in your stomach during a conversation with someone you are romantically involved with? Maybe it was a comment that did not sit right or a pattern of behavior that left you uneasy. Recognizing red flags in romantic relationships is not just about trusting your gut; it is about understanding what these signals can mean and how they can affect your future with someone. In this chapter, we explore the subtle and sometimes not-so-subtle indicators that can tell you a lot about a person's character and intentions. By learning to identify and respond to these red flags early, you can make informed decisions about whether to deepen the relationship or steer clear of it for your well-being.

6.1 Red Flags in Romantic Relationships

In the landscape of love and relationships, red flags are warning signs that the person you are with may not be conducive to a healthy, supportive partnership. These warnings can manifest in various behaviors that, when ignored, can lead to emotional distress or unhealthy relational dynamics. Let us discuss some specific behaviors that are considered red flags in romantic relationships: excessive jealousy, quick involvement, disrespect toward boundaries, and inconsistent communication.

Excessive jealousy, for instance, is often romanticized in media as a sign of deep affection or love. However, in reality, it signals insecurity and a desire for control rather than love. It can manifest as your partner getting upset when you spend time with other people or accusing you of being unfaithful without reason. This behavior strains the relationship and can isolate you from loved ones as you attempt to avoid conflicts. You must remember that jealousy does not equate to love.

Quick involvement in a relationship can also be a red flag. While it is flattering when someone expresses a lot of interest in you right from the start, accelerating the natural pace of a relationship can indicate issues with impulse control or a disregard for your comfort levels. For example, someone who pushes for an exclusive relationship after just a few dates or insists on moving in together quickly might not respect the time you need to make comfortable, considered decisions. This should definitely make you reconsider the speed of the relationship and what feels comfortable to you.

Disrespect towards boundaries is another critical red flag. Boundaries are fundamental to any healthy relationship. They can range from how much time you need alone to how you handle finances and personal space. A partner who repeatedly ignores or challenges your boundaries is demonstrating a lack of respect for your needs and autonomy. This might look like someone who uses guilt to coax you into decisions or who dismisses your feelings when you express discomfort or disagreement.

Inconsistent communication can indicate a lack of commitment or interest in the relationship. This behavior often needs to be clarified, leaving you questioning where you stand or what to expect next. For example, someone who is communicative and affectionate one day but distant and cold the next may be emotionally manipulating you to keep you on edge and more attached to their every whim. This could be an early red flag leading to codependency in the relationship.

Real-life Scenario: Recognizing Red Flags

Imagine Sarah, who recently started dating someone she met through friends. Initially, her partner was attentive and seemed genuinely interested in her life. However, over time, Sarah noticed that her partner would get overly upset whenever she spent time with her male friends. He justified his behavior by claiming his jealousy was just a sign of how much he cared for her. Additionally, he started making plans for them without consulting her, like booking a weekend getaway after just a few weeks of dating. Sarah felt overwhelmed and uncomfortable with the speed at which things were moving, but she initially mistook her discomfort in the relationship for typical new relationship nerves, thereby overlooking the red flag.

Advice on Immediate Actions

If you find yourself in a situation similar to Sarah's, addressing these red flags early is important. Communicate your feelings and concerns clearly. For example, you might say, "I appreciate your interest in our relationship, but I need more time to make decisions about big commitments." Setting and enforcing boundaries early on can help you gauge whether the other person respects your needs and is willing to adapt their behavior.

If the behavior continues despite your efforts, it may be necessary to reconsider the relationship's future. A relationship should enhance your life, not complicate it with doubts and discomfort. Trusting your instincts and taking action early can prevent deeper emotional investment in a potentially harmful relationship and a lot of wasted time.

Navigating romantic relationships requires a balance of heart and mindfulness. By staying alert to red flags and understanding their implications, you can protect your emotional well-being and foster relationships that are genuinely supportive and fulfilling. Remember, it is not just about finding someone; it is about finding the right someone who respects and enhances your life.

6.2 Warning Signs in Friendships and Work Relationships

When we think about all the relationships that shape our lives, it is not just the romantic partnerships that hold weight. Friendships and professional relationships are equally pivotal, influencing everything from our social satisfaction to our career trajectories. However, just like in romantic relationships, there are warning signs in these non-romantic interactions that can signal unhealthy dynamics. Recognizing these signs early can help you manage these relationships more effectively and protect your mental well-being.

In friendships, one significant red flag is constant one-upmanship. This can manifest when a friend must always outdo your experiences or achievements. If you share a success, they might immediately counter with a more significant success of their own or diminish yours. This behavior breeds a competitive atmosphere and undermines the supportive foundation upon which friendships should be built. Similarly, a lack of empathy—where a friend consistently shows little regard for your feelings or dismisses your problems—can signify a deeper issue in the friendship. It can leave you feeling unsupported and undervalued, which are feelings that have no place in a healthy friendship.

In the workplace, gossiping and undermining achievements are red flags that can disrupt your professional environment and career progression. Gossiping, especially when it is malicious or pervasive, can create a toxic atmosphere and lead to mistrust among colleagues. If you find that your achievements are often downplayed or stolen by a coworker, it could indicate a competitive or hostile work environment. These behaviors affect your job satisfaction and can impede your professional growth by skewing others' perceptions of your capabilities and undermining your contributions.

These behaviors in both personal and professional contexts can have severe impacts on your life. Constant competition and lack of support in friendships can lead to stress and self-doubt, making it difficult to enjoy social interactions and maintain self-esteem. In professional settings, gossip and undermining can create a hostile work environment, leading to job dissatisfaction, reduced productivity, and even career stagnation. Recognizing these red flags early is crucial for taking steps to manage these relationships effectively and maintain your overall mental health.

To distinguish between genuinely supportive interactions and those that are toxic or undermining, consider how you feel during and after those interactions. Healthy interactions generally leave you feeling uplifted, supported, and respected. In contrast, toxic interactions often leave you feeling drained, anxious, or upset. For instance, a supportive friend will celebrate your successes with genuine happiness and offer comfort or constructive advice during tough times. A supportive colleague will respect your contributions and collaborate with you to achieve shared goals rather than compete or steal credit.

Managing relationships with toxic friends or coworkers involves setting clear boundaries and, in some cases, limiting or ending interactions. If a friend consistently exhibits behaviors like one-upmanship or lack of empathy, address these issues directly. You might say, "I've noticed that our conversations often turn competitive, and it makes me uncomfortable. I value our friendship and would love for us to support each other more." If the behavior continues despite your efforts, it might be necessary to distance yourself from the relationship to protect your well-being.

In professional environments, document instances of undermining or inappropriate behavior, as these records can be helpful if you need to escalate the issue to human resources. Additionally, seek allies within your workplace who share your values and can provide support. Sometimes, having colleagues who acknowledge the situation can reduce the feeling of isolation and help you navigate the challenges more effectively.

By staying vigilant and proactive about managing these non-romantic relationships, you can create a personal and professional life that is not only successful but also supportive and fulfilling. Recognizing and addressing these red flags protects your mental health and empowers you to build and maintain healthier, more constructive relationships.

6.3 Trusting Your Gut: Intuition and Red Flags

Intuition plays a pivotal role in our lives, particularly when it comes to navigating personal relationships. Often referred to as a 'gut feeling,' intuition is that instinctive awareness or understanding that we cannot always rationalize but strongly feel. It develops within us over time and experience. In the context of relationships, intuition can serve as an early warning system—an internal alert that signals when something might not be right, even before we fully understand why. This subtle yet potent internal guide can help us recognize red flags that our conscious mind might overlook or rationalize away.

Understanding the value of intuition in recognizing red flags requires acknowledging that our subconscious can pick up on inconsistencies and deceptive behaviors before our rational mind catches up. For instance, you might feel uneasy about someone's sincerity even if they have not done anything overtly deceptive. This discomfort may stem from non-verbal cues such as avoiding eye contact, inconsistencies in their stories, or even their tone when speaking about sensitive topics. These signals can be subtle, and it is your intuition that processes these minute details and signals a warning. It is important to heed this warning system early on when it is triggered.

However, distinguishing between intuition and irrational fear is crucial. Fear is an emotional response that is often based on past experiences, insecurities, or personal biases—it can lead to defensive reactions that are not necessarily reflective of the present situation. Intuition, on the other hand, is a calm but persistent awareness that something in the environment is off. It does not provoke anxiety or panic but rather a steady sense of caution. To differentiate between the two, assess your feelings objectively: Are your reactions based on present facts, or are they influenced by past traumas or generalized anxieties? If your concern is consistently focused on specific behaviors or patterns that feel misaligned with your values or expectations, it is likely your intuition speaking.

Strengthening your intuitive senses can enhance your ability to detect red flags early in any interpersonal interaction. One effective way to do this is through mindfulness practices. Mindfulness involves staying present and fully engaged in the current moment, which can heighten your awareness of the subtleties in people's behaviors and your environment. Regular meditation can also sharpen your intuition by calming the mind, reducing noise from incessant thoughts and fears, and allowing you to recognize better and trust your gut feelings. Additionally, paying attention to your physical reactions during interactions can provide clues; often, our bodies react to discomfort before our minds are consciously aware of it. A sudden tightness in your chest or a knot in your stomach during certain interactions can be significant indicators that something is amiss and should not be ignored.

Another vital aspect of trusting your intuition is validating these feelings. Discussing your perceptions with trusted friends, family members, or a counselor can provide an external perspective that helps confirm or challenge your instincts. This validation is especially important because it can either reassure you that your instincts are based on observable behaviors or help you realize that unrelated personal issues or anxieties might influence your feelings.

Encouraging this kind of introspection and dialogue about intuition and its role in identifying red flags in relationships empowers you to trust your instincts. It also enhances your ability to act on them appropriately. By cultivating an attentive and mindful approach to how you feel in various social and personal interactions, you equip yourself with a subtle yet powerful tool that guides you toward healthier and more fulfilling relationships. Remember, your intuition is a profound part of your cognitive toolkit, and honing this skill can provide you with an invaluable protective mechanism in navigating the complex world of human relationships.

6.4 Constructive Responses to Red Flags

When you notice red flags in any of your relationships, whether they are personal or professional, the initial steps you take can significantly influence the outcomes. It is essential to address these concerns constructively and calmly to ensure that your concerns are heard and taken seriously. Let us explore how you can approach these situations with clarity and tact, setting the stage for a resolution that respects your boundaries and well-being.

The first step in addressing red flags is to communicate your concerns clearly and calmly. This might seem daunting, especially if you are worried about confrontation or your previous attempts have not been taken seriously. However, clear communication is crucial in ensuring that the other party understands your perspective and the seriousness of your concerns. It is helpful to approach this conversation with specific examples of the behavior that has troubled you, as this can prevent the discussion from becoming too abstract or emotional. For instance, if you are dealing with a partner who is dismissive of your feelings, you might say, "I feel hurt when I share my feelings about my day, and you change the subject quickly. It makes me feel like my experiences are not important to you. Can we discuss this further?" By focusing on your feelings and the direct impact of their actions, you aim to encourage a more empathetic response and a constructive conversation.

In scenarios where personal discussions have failed or are not advisable, such as in a professional environment with a superior, involving a mediator can be beneficial. Mediators, whether they are HR representatives in a workplace or mutual friends in personal relationships, can provide an objective perspective and facilitate a dialogue that might be difficult to manage alone. They can help clarify misunderstandings, mediate differences, and propose solutions that respect both parties' needs. When choosing to involve a mediator, it is essential to select someone who is impartial and respected by both parties to maintain the trust and openness required for an effective mediation.

Documentation plays a critical role in managing red flags, especially in environments where the issues might escalate or where you might need to substantiate your claims, such as in the workplace. Keeping a record of incidents that exemplify the red flags helps in discussions with mediators. It serves as a personal reminder of the realities of the situation, which can sometimes become blurred under emotional stress or manipulation. This might include saving emails and messages, keeping a journal of incidents, or noting dates and details of specific occurrences. For example, if you are dealing with a coworker who regularly takes credit for your work, documenting the instances and any tangible evidence, like emails, can be crucial in presenting your case to HR.

In any scenario, whether addressing red flags in personal or professional relationships, the key is to act from a place of informed strength and resolve. By clearly communicating your concerns, involving mediators when necessary, and keeping detailed records, you equip yourself with the tools needed to address and resolve these issues effectively. These strategies help manage immediate situations and contribute to a broader understanding of protecting your interests and maintaining healthy boundaries in all areas of your life.

6.5 When to Stay and When to Walk Away

Making the decision whether to stay in a relationship or to walk away is perhaps one of the most pivotal choices you might face. It is a decision that affects your immediate emotional well-being and sets the course for your future happiness and sense of self. When faced with red flags, understanding when they signal a need for a direct exit or an opportunity for resolution is crucial. This framework is designed to help you navigate these often murky waters, ensuring that your decisions are well-informed, respectful to your needs, and lead to a healthier life path.

Firstly, evaluating the severity and frequency of the red flags you are encountering is essential. Severity refers to the impact of the behavior on your emotional, physical, and psychological health. For instance, behaviors that threaten your safety or lead to persistent psychological distress are of high severity. Frequency, on the other hand, considers how often these behaviors occur. Is the troubling behavior a rare occurrence or a consistent pattern? For example, a partner who occasionally becomes slightly overbearing might require a different approach compared to one who regularly exhibits controlling behaviors that leave you feeling trapped or demeaned.

Assessing these factors requires honest reflection. You might find it helpful to write down instances of concerning behavior, noting how often they occur and how they affect you. This record can help you visualize the dynamics of the relationship more clearly and guide your decision-making process. If you find that high-severity behaviors are frequent, it may be a strong indicator that the relationship is fundamentally unhealthy, and remaining in it could be detrimental to your overall happiness and well-being.

The priority of your personal safety and happiness cannot be overstressed. In any relationship, your well-being should be paramount. Read that again; your well-being should be paramount. If staying in a relationship means consistently putting your needs, safety, or happiness aside, it may be time to reconsider your involvement. It is essential to recognize that while relationships involve compromise, they should not involve sacrificing your fundamental well-being.

For those who decide that leaving is the necessary course of action, especially in scenarios where safety is a concern, it is critical to have access to resources that can facilitate a safe exit. Organizations such as the National Domestic Violence Hotline in the United States offer confidential advice and support. Additionally, local shelters and services can provide immediate help and safety planning. Preparing a safety plan, which might include saving money, having a packed bag ready, and arranging a place to stay, can make the process of leaving safer and more manageable.

Communication is vital in cases where the red flags are not severe or frequent, and you feel that the relationship has room for growth. Addressing concerns openly and honestly can pave the way for improvements. However, it is essential to set clear expectations for change and to be mindful of whether actual progress is being made over time. If the relationship shows no signs of improvement despite your efforts, or if the same issues continue to resurface, it may be a sign that it is time to walk away.

Navigating the complexities of when to stay or leave requires a delicate balance of introspection, communication, and, sometimes, the courage to make tough decisions. By assessing the severity and frequency of issues, prioritizing your safety and happiness, and utilizing available resources, you can make choices that respect your well-being and steer you toward healthier and more fulfilling relationships.

As we wrap up this chapter, remember that recognizing when to stay or walk away is not just about managing relationships—it is about managing your life and steering it toward safety, happiness, and health. This decision-making process is integral to cultivating self-respect and building the life you deserve.

Looking ahead into the next chapter, we will focus on healing and rebuilding after leaving a toxic relationship. It is about turning new pages and planting seeds for a renewed life that respects your worth and cherishes your well-being.

CHAPTER 7
HEALING FROM PAST TOXIC RELATIONSHIPS

H as the echo of a past relationship left you wondering if the pain and confusion will ever fade? This question, while deeply unsettling, is a common thread among those who have stepped away from toxic relationships. Much like the breakdown that precedes it, the phase of healing is intense and all-consuming, and understanding this process is pivotal in navigating the path to recovery.

7.1 Understanding the Healing Process

Healing from a toxic relationship is a journey that often feels more like a roller coaster of emotions rather than a straightforward path. Recognizing the stages you might go through can provide a roadmap, helping you to understand and normalize what you feel at each step. Initially, denial often sets in as the first protective layer. It is not uncommon to downplay the relationship's negative aspects or the impact it has on you. You might catch yourself thinking, "It wasn't that bad," or even questioning whether it was toxic at all. This is your defense mechanism, underplaying the true negativities you encountered.

Following the denial, anger frequently surfaces. This anger can be directed toward your former partner, yourself, or even external situations you perceive as having kept you in the relationship. It is a fiery stage that burns with questions of 'why' and 'how,' serving as a cathartic release of bottled-up frustrations.

Bargaining may come next, where you find yourself ruminating over what could have been done differently. "If only I had spoken up sooner" or "What if I had left earlier?" are thoughts that might play on repeat, indicating a struggle to accept the past as it is. This stage can be particularly painful because it intertwines hope with regret, making it difficult to let go.

Depression often follows as the total weight of the loss and its implications settle in. It is a quiet, introspective phase, marked not by sadness alone but by a deep sense of loss—loss of what you invested, what you hoped for, and even parts of your identity that were tied up in the relationship. It is essential to know that this process is fluid, and you may find yourself moving forward or backward.

Acceptance is the stage that brings gentle relief. It does not negate the past pain but allows you to see it without being overwhelmed by it. Acceptance involves acknowledging the reality of the relationship and its end as part of your life's narrative but not its defining feature. You now understand that your past does not dictate your future.

It is crucial to emphasize that healing is not a linear process. You might find yourself revisiting anger after you thought acceptance had settled in or slipping back into bargaining on difficult days.

This non-linearity is not a sign of failing to heal but a normal part of the human psychological experience when processing deep emotional wounds.

Self-awareness plays a critical role throughout these stages. You can navigate the healing process more effectively by becoming attuned to your emotions and reactions. Recognizing when you are slipping into denial or becoming stuck in bargaining allows you to address these feelings consciously, perhaps through therapy or reflective practices like journaling.

Setting realistic expectations for your healing journey is also vital. Healing takes time, and the duration varies significantly from one person to another. Patience and self-compassion are your allies here. Allow yourself to feel without judgment, give yourself permission to heal at your own pace, and remember that each step is progress, no matter how small.

Interactive Element: Reflective Journaling Prompt

Consider keeping a healing journal. Regular entries can help you track your progress through these stages, reflect on your feelings, and recognize patterns or triggers. Here is a prompt to get you started: "Today, I felt ___ because ___. In this moment, I choose to ___ to support my healing." This simple practice can be profoundly supportive in fostering self-awareness and patience with your healing process.

Understanding these stages and aspects of the healing process provides a foundation for the emotional work required to move forward. While the journey is undoubtedly challenging, gaining clarity on what to expect and how to manage each phase can empower you to navigate your healing with greater confidence and self-compassion. As you continue to move through these stages, remember that healing is about getting back to where you were before and growing into who you are meant to become— stronger, wiser, and fully capable of fostering healthy, fulfilling relationships in the future.

7.2 Techniques for Emotional Healing

When you are on the path to recovery from the remnants of a toxic relationship, embracing various emotional healing techniques can be transformative. These techniques, from mindfulness meditation to expressive writing and creative arts therapies, offer you tools to cope, thrive, and rediscover your inner strength. Each of these approaches has its unique way of facilitating emotional release, fostering self-understanding, and reducing the stress that often lingers after difficult experiences.

Mindfulness meditation is a powerful practice that teaches you to focus on the present moment while acknowledging and accepting your feelings, thoughts, and bodily sensations without judgment. This practice can be particularly beneficial if you find yourself ruminating on past events or anxieties about the future, common issues following toxic relationships. By bringing your attention back to the present, mindfulness helps decrease stress and anxiety, enhances emotional resilience, and improves overall mental focus. To integrate mindfulness into your daily routine, start with just a few minutes each day. Find a quiet space, sit comfortably, close your eyes, and focus on your breath. When your mind wanders, gently bring your attention back to your breathing. Gradually increase the duration as you become more comfortable with the practice.

Expressive writing, another potent healing tool, involves writing down your deepest thoughts and feelings about the experiences you have gone through. This practice can help you process emotions that might be too painful to speak about and can lead to a significant reduction in emotional distress. It is a way to declutter your mind, make sense of your experiences, and gain clarity. To begin, **set aside a few minutes each day to write in a private journal.** Write continuously about how you feel without worrying about punctuation or grammar. The key is to let your thoughts flow without censorship or judgment, which can lead to profound insights and emotional catharsis.

Creative arts therapies, including art, music, and dance therapy, offer expressive tools to help you communicate feelings that might be difficult to articulate verbally. Engaging in artistic activities can reduce stress, alleviate depression, and improve self-esteem. For instance, painting or drawing allows you to express emotions through colors and shapes, visually representing your feelings. Music therapy can include playing instruments, singing, or even listening to music that resonates with your emotions, facilitating a therapeutic release. Dance therapy involves using body movements to express feelings, which can be particularly cathartic and empowering. To incorporate these therapies into your life, you might start by attending a class or simply dedicating some time at home to engage in these creative expressions. The key is to focus on the process of creation without judgment about the outcome.

Making these practices a regular part of your life is crucial for their effectiveness. Consistency helps establish these techniques as coping mechanisms you can rely on whenever you feel overwhelmed. Over time, they become more than just recovery tools; they transform into integral components of your daily self-care routine, continuously supporting your emotional well-being.

By embracing these varied techniques, you equip yourself with a robust set of tools to manage and move beyond the emotional challenges left in the wake of toxic relationships. Each approach offers unique benefits that contribute to a holistic healing process, reinforcing your journey toward a happier, healthier self. As you explore and integrate these practices, you may find that they not only help in healing but also enrich your overall quality of life, opening up new avenues for joy and self-expression that were previously overshadowed by past pains.

7.3 The Role of Therapy and Support Groups

When the echoes of a toxic relationship still reverberate through your daily life, seeking professional help can be a transformative step towards profound healing and understanding. Therapy, in its various forms, offers not just relief but also strategies for managing the complex emotions and unresolved trauma that can linger long after the relationship has ended. The beauty of therapy lies in its ability to provide a safe, confidential space where you can explore your deepest feelings without judgment. Here, with a professional, you can start to dissect the impact your experiences have had on you, unraveling the tightly wound threads of confusion, guilt, or self-doubt that past interactions may have instilled.

Cognitive-behavioral therapy (CBT), one of the most widely recognized therapeutic approaches, is particularly effective for those recovering from toxic relationships. CBT focuses on identifying and challenging negative thought patterns and behaviors, aiming to replace them with healthier, more constructive ones. This approach is hands-on and practical, making it an excellent choice for addressing the immediate, distressing symptoms that can arise from toxic encounters, such as intrusive thoughts or persistent self-blame. Through CBT, you can learn to recognize triggers that may provoke emotional responses based on past traumas and develop coping strategies that empower you to regain control over your reactions.

Trauma-focused therapy is another approach that delves deeper into the emotional scars left by toxic relationships. This form of therapy acknowledges that trauma can profoundly affect your mental health and seeks to address the root causes of this distress. It involves various techniques, such as exposure therapy or eye movement desensitization and reprocessing (EMDR), which are designed to help you process and make sense of your traumatic experiences in a controlled, therapeutic setting. By confronting these memories in a safe space, trauma-focused therapy aims to diminish their power over your present life.

Group therapy offers a different but equally valuable therapeutic experience. In these sessions, you engage with others who have faced similar challenges, sharing stories and solutions in a structured environment facilitated by a therapist. This setting can be incredibly validating and comforting, as it helps dismantle the isolation that often accompanies the aftermath of toxic relationships. Hearing that others have experienced similar emotions and challenges can be profoundly reassuring, and the communal support can foster a sense of belonging and collective healing. This type of group therapy lets you know you are not alone in your healing journey.

Finding the right therapist or support group is crucial to making your therapeutic journey effective. When looking for a therapist, consider their specialization and whether it aligns with your needs—someone who understands the dynamics of toxic relationships and has experience in dealing with similar cases can be particularly beneficial. It is also essential to feel a personal connection with your therapist; therapy is a deeply personal process, and feeling comfortable and understood by your therapist is paramount. Do not hesitate to meet with a few therapists before deciding on one you feel genuinely comfortable with.

When searching for a support group, look for one that maintains a positive, constructive focus rather than merely a space for sharing grievances. You can gather tools in your therapy sessions to overcome the feelings of isolation and stress caused by toxic relationships. Effective support groups should feel safe and inclusive, providing a balance of sharing, listening, and mutual support under professional guidance. Questions to ask before joining might include the group's structure, the typical session format, and how the group ensures a safe environment for all members.

Engaging in therapy or joining a support group can significantly aid your recovery from the impacts of toxic relationships, providing tools and insights that foster healing and growth. As you explore these options, remember that taking this step is not a sign of weakness but a profound act of strength and self-care, marking an important phase in your journey toward reclaiming your life and emotional well-being.

7.4 Forgiving Yourself and Others

Forgiveness is often viewed through the lens of restoring relationships or offering absolution to others. However, in the context of healing from toxic relationships, forgiveness assumes a more personal and transformative role. It is about releasing yourself from the chains of ongoing resentment and anger that, while justified, can hinder your healing and personal growth. This process is less about exonerating those who have wronged you and more about giving yourself the peace and freedom to move forward.

Forgiving oneself is an essential part of this process. Many individuals harbor deep-seated guilt and self-blame for their role in a toxic relationship. You might criticize yourself for not recognizing the signs earlier, for staying too long, or for the compromises you made that went against your better judgment. These feelings, while natural, can act as barriers to self-compassion and recovery. To begin the journey of self-forgiveness, it is crucial to understand that you acted with the knowledge and resources you had at the time. Reflecting on this can gradually shift your perspective, helping you recognize that your actions were based on your understanding and capacities in those moments. Strategies to foster self-forgiveness include writing yourself a letter of forgiveness, speaking affirmations that reinforce your inherent worth, or engaging in meditative practices that focus on self-compassion. Each of these activities provides a space to work through feelings of guilt and self-blame, reinforcing your acceptance of the past and your commitment to moving forward into a brighter future.

Forgiving those who have caused you harm in a toxic relationship is another challenging yet vital step. Begin by acknowledging the full extent of your hurt without minimization. Recognizing how deeply you were affected is not about dwelling on the pain but about validating your feelings and experiences. Understanding the context of the other person's behavior can also be insightful. Often, those who perpetuate toxicity are themselves repeating patterns they have learned or responding to their insecurities and traumas. This does not excuse their behaviors, but understanding these aspects can sometimes make forgiveness feel more accessible. The next step involves emotionally letting go, a process that might require you to actively decide to release the hold this pain has on your life. Techniques such as visualization—imagining the weight of your hurt lifting off your shoulders—or writing a goodbye letter to your pain can be symbolic gestures of letting go.

It is essential to clarify that forgiveness does not necessarily mean reconciliation. You can forgive someone and still choose to maintain distance or cut ties entirely for your well-being. Setting this boundary is a critical aspect of forgiveness, underscoring that your decision to forgive is primarily for your peace and healing. It is about reclaiming your emotional space and energy, redirecting it towards more positive, uplifting areas of your life. In this sense, forgiveness is a profound act of self-care and empowerment—a step towards liberating yourself from the emotional ties that bind you to the past.

Navigating forgiveness is a deeply personal and often complex process that unfolds in its own time. It requires patience, courage, and an ongoing commitment to your healing and well-being. As you embark on this path, remember that each step towards forgiveness, be it forgiving yourself or others, is a step towards a lighter, more liberated existence. It allows you to close a painful chapter and open up to new possibilities of joy and fulfillment, unencumbered by the weight of past hurts.

7.5 Rebuilding Trust in Relationships

After stepping away from a toxic relationship, it is not uncommon to find that your trust in others, and crucially, in yourself, has been shaken. This erosion of trust can cast a long shadow, affecting how you interact with new people and coloring your perceptions of their intentions. Yet, trust is the scaffold on which all healthy relationships are built—it is fundamental to establishing connections that are both fulfilling and supportive. The good news is that trust, much like a skill, can be rebuilt through conscious effort and deliberate practice.

The first step in this rebuilding process is focusing on self-trust. In toxic relationships, your instincts and judgments were likely undermined or dismissed, leading to a point where trusting your decisions became fraught with doubt. To regain confidence in your own judgment, start small. Make daily decisions independently and reflect on the outcomes. These do not have to be monumental choices; they can be as simple as deciding where to go for a walk or what movie to watch. The goal is to reinforce your ability to trust your own instincts without external validation from anyone other than yourself. As your confidence grows with these smaller decisions, gradually increase the stakes, trusting yourself to make more significant choices about your life and relationships.

Once you feel more grounded in your self-trust, you can begin to extend trust cautiously to others. This process should be slow and measured. Begin by setting small, testable trust challenges for people in your life. For example, you might ask a friend to keep a minor secret or rely on a new colleague to handle a component of a project. The key here is to start with low-risk situations where the potential for disappointment is manageable. Each time your trust is honored, it reinforces your belief in your ability to judge character and intent, slowly extending your comfort zone.

However, maintaining a balance between trust and healthy skepticism is essential. While it is important to open yourself up to trusting relationships, it is equally important to protect yourself from potential harm. This balance can be achieved by listening to your instincts and watching for red flags, much like you would monitor any other emotional responses in relationships. If someone consistently meets the small trust challenges you set but something still feels off, it is worth taking a closer step to understand why. Sometimes, our subconscious picks up on cues before our conscious mind does. Trusting your gut means giving weight to these feelings and exploring them further rather than just dismissing them outright.

As you navigate these steps, remember that the goal is not to shield yourself behind impenetrable walls but to build a gateway through which the right people—those who respect and honor your trust—can enter. By gradually extending trust and observing how it is handled, you create a filter that separates those who will enhance your life from those who may detract from it. This selective trust-building protects you from future toxic relationships and enriches your life with positive, supportive interactions.

In essence, rebuilding trust is about finding the sweet spot between openness and caution. It is about learning to trust again, not just in others but also in your capacity to foster and nurture healthy and rewarding relationships. As you apply these steps and strategies, you will find that trust, like a well-tended garden, grows and strengthens over time, forming the foundation of relationships that are not only safe for you to grow and thrive but also deeply fulfilling.

CHAPTER 8
BUILDING HEALTHY RELATIONSHIPS

I sn't it remarkable how the sturdiest buildings require a solid foundation to withstand the tests of time? Similarly, the healthiest relationships rely on fundamental components that ensure their longevity and resilience. As we explore the foundations of a healthy relationship, consider this a blueprint—a guide to building and nurturing relationships that not only endure but flourish.

8.1 Foundations of a Healthy Relationship

Identifying Core Components

The core components of trust, honesty, empathy, and mutual support lie at the heart of every thriving relationship. These elements act like the four corners of a strong foundation, each playing a crucial role in the relationship's overall stability and health.

- **Trust** is perhaps the cornerstone of this foundation. It is built over time through consistent actions and reliability. When trust is present, partners feel secure in the relationship, knowing they can rely on each other without fear of betrayal.
- **Honesty** complements trust, providing the transparency necessary for maintaining it. Open and truthful communication fosters a deeper understanding and prevents misunderstandings that could erode trust.
- **Empathy** involves understanding and sharing your partner's feelings. It allows you to see situations from your partner's perspective and respond with compassion and support, strengthening the bond between you.
- **Mutual support**, the final cornerstone, involves standing by each other during challenges and pursuing personal ambitions and joys. It celebrates successes and provides comfort during hardships, acting as a critical support system for individual and relational growth.

Role of Individual Health

A healthy relationship is not just about how well partners relate to each other but also about how well each person relates to themselves. Individual health, particularly mental and emotional wellness, plays a significant role in the relationship's dynamics. Engaging in self-care practices, addressing personal mental health issues, and maintaining an individual sense of well-being are all essential. A partnership where both individuals are mentally and emotionally healthy tends to be more balanced and less prone to codependency, allowing for a relationship that enhances each person's life and endures the test of time.

Importance of Shared Values and Goals

Shared values and goals act as the beams that support the structure of a relationship, providing direction and a common purpose. Whether it is family planning, career goals, or personal values such as honesty and kindness, these shared elements offer a sense of unity and partnership. They guide decision-making and conflict resolution, providing a common ground that can help navigate through the complexities of life together. Moreover, aligning on these critical aspects of life ensures that both partners are moving in the same direction, each step forward bringing them closer rather than driving a wedge between them.

Flexibility and Adaptability

Just as buildings must be flexible enough to withstand forces without breaking, relationships require flexibility and adaptability to thrive amidst life's changes and challenges. This means being open to growth as individuals and as a couple and being willing to adjust plans and dreams as needed. Flexibility in a relationship might look like adjusting your expectations or being open to new communication methods. It allows the relationship to evolve, adapting to each partner's growth and changes in circumstances. It helps manage conflicts more effectively, as both partners are more willing to explore solutions beyond their comfort zones.

Reflective Exercise: Evaluating Your Relationship's Foundation

To further understand the strength of your relationship's foundation, take some time to reflect on the following questions:

- How often do I feel I can truly trust my partner?

- Are honesty and transparency consistently practiced in our relationship?
- Do I feel empathized with and supported in my endeavors?
- Are our values and goals in alignment, and how do we handle differences?

This exercise is about identifying areas that may need improvement and appreciating the aspects of your relationship that are thriving. Recognizing both strengths and weaknesses can guide you in nurturing and fortifying your relationship, ensuring it remains strong and healthy.

As you contemplate these foundational elements, remember that every relationship is unique, and building a healthy one is not about achieving perfection but about striving for a balanced, fulfilling partnership. Each step taken to strengthen these core components is a step towards a more robust and resilient relationship that not only survives life's challenges but also provides a source of joy and support.

8.2 Communication Skills for Relationship Success

Communication is often likened to the bloodstream of a relationship, essential for the vitality and health of the connection between partners. Effective communication involves more than just talking and listening; it encompasses understanding, respect, and a mutual effort to foster closeness and understanding. Engaging in clear and open communication involves several key techniques that can significantly enhance the quality of your interactions.

One foundational technique is **active listening**, which involves fully concentrating on what is being said rather than passively hearing the message of your partner. This technique ensures that you are genuinely engaged in the conversation and helps you understand the underlying emotions and intentions. Active listening also manifests through nonverbal cues such as nodding, maintaining eye contact, and mirroring the speaker's emotions, all of which signal that you are fully present and involved. Another powerful tool in effective communication is using "**I" statements**. This approach involves framing your thoughts and feelings from your perspective without placing blame or judgment on your partner. For example, saying, "I feel hurt when plans are canceled at the last minute" instead of "You don't care about our plans," can reduce defensiveness, opens the lines of communication, and provide space for understanding and resolution.

Regular, uninterrupted 'check-ins' are another essential aspect of healthy communication. These are dedicated times you and your partner agree to discuss your feelings, thoughts, and experiences. Whether daily or weekly, these check-ins can prevent minor misunderstandings from becoming more significant conflicts and help maintain a solid emotional connection. During these sessions, both partners have an equal opportunity to express themselves openly and honestly, fostering a culture of transparency and mutual respect.

Handling conflicts constructively is equally important and requires specific skills that ensure disagreements do not escalate into resentment or lasting conflict. One effective method is to focus on the issue at hand rather than attacking your partner's character or dredging up past mistakes. This approach keeps the discussion productive and solution-focused. Additionally, recognizing when a conversation escalates into an argument allows you to propose a pause. Taking a break when emotions run high can prevent hurtful words and ensure both partners have the space to cool down and approach the issue with a clearer mind.

Encouraging vulnerability in a relationship opens deeper levels of intimacy and trust. Sharing your fears, hopes, and insecurities can seem daunting, but it is a profound way to strengthen your bond. When one partner is vulnerable, it often invites the other to share more freely, creating a cycle of openness and trust. However, it is essential to ensure that the environment is safe for such disclosures. Reacting with empathy, withholding judgment, and offering support when your partner shares something personal are all ways to encourage a safe and supportive space for vulnerability.

Finally, the ability to give and receive feedback constructively is a skill that can transform how you grow both individually and as a couple. Constructive feedback involves clear, specific comments focusing on behaviors rather than personality traits. For instance, saying, "I appreciate it when you help with house chores without me asking," is more effective than vague praise. Similarly, when receiving feedback from someone, try to listen openly without becoming defensive. View feedback as an opportunity to better understand your partner's needs and preferences, not as criticism or a personal attack on your character.

By integrating these communication skills into your daily interactions, you lay a strong foundation for a relationship characterized by mutual respect, understanding, and continuous growth. Each conversation becomes an opportunity to deepen your connection, resolve differences, and build a lasting partnership based on mutual trust and understanding.

8.3 Respect and Love: Pillars of Healthy Partnerships

When you think about the foundations of a lasting partnership, respect, and love might rightfully come to mind first. These elements shape every interaction and decision within a relationship, creating an environment that either nurtures growth or stifles it. To truly respect and love someone means more than mere declarations; it is shown in daily actions, respect for boundaries, sincere appreciation, and support for each person's individuality.

Respect in action means listening attentively when your partner speaks, valuing their opinions even when they differ from yours, and treating their aspirations with as much regard as you would your own. It is also found in the smaller gestures—acknowledging their efforts, saying 'thank you,' and being mindful of their preferences in your day-to-day life. Moreover, respecting boundaries is paramount. This is not just about physical or digital boundaries but also emotional ones. It involves understanding and agreeing on what is shared and what is kept private, what is open for discussion, and what is off-limits. This mutual respect ensures that each person feels safe and valued, not just for what they contribute to the relationship but for who they are as individuals.

In its truest form, love is an active and dynamic force in a relationship. It is about showing up for one another, especially during challenging times. It is about the encouragement given without a second thought, the comfort offered without reservation, and the joy shared in each other's successes. Love is not just about supporting each other on the bad days but also about lifting each other higher on the good days. It is a commitment to mutual growth and happiness rooted in deeply understanding each other's needs and dreams.

Maintaining individual identities within a relationship is crucial. It is easy to become so intertwined with another person that you lose sight of who you are by yourself and your individuality. Healthy relationships recognize and celebrate individuality; they encourage personal pursuits and hobbies without jealousy or insecurity. Supporting your partner's interests and personal endeavors, even when they do not involve you, is a testament to a love that is secure and self-assured. This respect for personal space and identity not only strengthens the relationship but also enriches the lives of each partner, allowing them to bring new experiences and energy back into the partnership.

Equality and partnership stand at the core of any balanced relationship. This means that decisions, responsibilities, and power are shared. It is not about one leading and the other following, but both partners walking side by side, each having an equal say in the direction of their shared life. This balance fosters a sense of fairness and mutual respect, where both partners feel their voices are heard and their contributions valued. It involves negotiation and compromise, recognizing that while one may not always agree, the process of reaching a decision is done with respect for the other's perspective.

Consistency and reliability are the bedrock of trust and security in a relationship. They transform the abstract concepts of love and respect into tangible experiences. Consistent actions—whether it is making time for each other, following through on promises, or showing up when it matters most—will build a foundation of dependability. When actions match words, trust will deepen, and love grows stronger. This reliability creates a safe space where both partners feel secure, not just in their relationship but also in their ability to face the world together, including any challenges that come their way.

By cultivating these aspects of respect and love, you create a healthy and strong relationship that is deeply satisfying and enriching. It becomes a partnership that nurtures and inspires, allowing you to flourish individually and as a couple.

8.4 Nurturing Positivity and Growth Together

In the dance of a lasting relationship, nurturing positivity and growth stands as a testament to the resilience and joy that two people can cultivate together. It is about focusing on what each person brings to the table—celebrating those contributions rather than fixating on shortcomings. Imagine your relationship as a garden where you and your partner are gardeners. By nurturing it with positivity, you are watering the plants, ensuring they thrive. Positive reinforcement and gratitude are your tools in this endeavor. When you actively acknowledge and appreciate the little things—like thanking your partner for their thoughtfulness or acknowledging their efforts in managing chores—it reinforces positive behaviors and nurtures a culture of appreciation and respect. This practice enhances your daily interactions and deepens the roots of your relationship, making it robust against the storms of conflict and misunderstanding.

Adopting a growth mindset within your relationship transforms challenges into stepping stones for personal and relational development. This perspective encourages you and your partner to see difficulties as opportunities to learn and grow rather than obstacles threatening your relationship. For instance, a disagreement over financial management could be approached as a chance to align on your financial goals and strategies rather than a battle to be won. Embracing this mindset involves recognizing that perfection is less important than progress and that every step forward, no matter how small, is valuable. It is about celebrating the evolution in your relationship with each other, which fosters a dynamic of continuous improvement and adaptation.

Shared experiences are the threads that weave the fabric of your relationship, adding strength and color to the tapestry of your shared life. Engaging in activities together, such as travel, hobbies, or attending cultural events, brings joy and excitement to your relationship and strengthens your bond. These experiences create memories that can remind you of your connection and the joys you have shared, especially when the relationship might face challenges. Whether it is a weekend getaway, a cooking class, or a concert, each shared experience enriches your relationship, providing common ground and a reservoir of happiness to draw from in less joyful times.

One of the most profound aspects of a strong partnership is supporting each other through personal challenges. It is about being there for each other, not just in times of external stress but also through internal struggles. Your support can be their stronghold when your partner faces challenges, whether professional setbacks, personal doubts, or emotional turmoil. Listening empathetically without immediately trying to fix the problem, offering reassurance when they doubt themselves, and standing by them as they navigate their way through these challenges, you become an irreplaceable pillar in their life. This support helps your partner through difficult times and strengthens the trust and gratitude in your relationship, reinforcing the idea that you can count on each other no matter what.

In cultivating these elements of positivity, growth, shared joy, and mutual support, you create a relationship that survives and thrives. It becomes a partnership where both individuals feel valued, understood, and supported, capable of facing both the challenges and celebrations life has to offer.

8.5 Recognizing and Celebrating Healthy Love

In the landscape of a thriving relationship, recognizing and celebrating the aspects of healthy love is akin to appreciating the vibrant colors in a well-tended garden. It is about noticing the hues of mutual respect, the fragrance of shared joy, and the texture of security and contentment that comes from genuinely harmonious companionship. These indicators are not just signs of a healthy relationship; they are the very essence that sustains and enriches it over time.

Mutual respect in a relationship manifests through consistently considering and valuing each other's opinions, feelings, and needs. It is seeing your partner as an equal, honoring their boundaries, and appreciating their contributions to your life. **Joy in each other's company** is another telling sign of healthy love. This joy does not stem merely from significant events or special occasions; it is present in the quiet moments, the everyday interactions that feel engaging and fulfilling. Lastly, a **general sense of security and contentment** indicates a solid foundation of trust and understanding, where both partners feel safe and valued, not just for what they do, but for who they are.

Celebrating milestones and achievements together is a crucial aspect of nurturing and maintaining the bond between partners. These celebrations can be as grand as a surprise party for a promotion or as simple as a quiet dinner at home to mark the end of a challenging week. The act of celebration does more than acknowledge an achievement; it reinforces the bond between you and your partner, creating shared memories that deepen your connection. It is a way of saying, "I see you; I appreciate you, and I am with you," which can significantly enhance the sense of partnership.

Renewing commitment to each other is equally important in keeping the relationship vibrant and strong. This does not necessarily mean grand gestures like renewing vows in a lavish ceremony—although those can certainly be meaningful. It can be as simple as setting aside time to reflect on your relationship and express your ongoing commitment to each other. This could involve writing a heartfelt note, planning a day to revisit the place where you first met, or just spending a quiet evening together, talking about your journey, and reiterating your dedication to the future. These acts of reaffirmation strengthen the emotional ties and remind both partners of their shared values and mutual commitment.

Continuous appreciation plays a pivotal role in a relationship's day-to-day health. It is about acknowledging the small gestures as much as the grand ones. A simple thank you for making coffee in the morning, a quick text to say you are thinking of each other during a busy day, or a compliment on how they handled a difficult situation can all contribute to a culture of appreciation and respect. These acknowledgments make each partner feel valued and appreciated, which fuels their investment in the relationship.

As we weave these threads of recognition, celebration, and reaffirmation into the fabric of our relationships, we not only enhance our current interactions but also lay the groundwork for enduring intimacy and connection. It is these elements that transform a good relationship into a great one, filled with respect, joy, and a deep, comforting sense of security.

In wrapping up this exploration of healthy relationships, remember that the beauty of love lies not just in the extraordinary moments but in the simple, everyday acts of kindness, respect, and appreciation. By fostering these elements, you cultivate a relationship that not only withstands the tests of time but also brings out the best in you and your partner. As we move forward, the next chapter will focus on strategies for resolving conflicts and navigating challenges, ensuring that your relationship continues to grow and thrive in the face of life's inevitable ups and downs.

CHAPTER 9

PREVENTATIVE STRATEGIES TO AVOID TOXIC RELATIONSHIPS

Have you ever found yourself in a familiar yet unwelcome dance with relationship dynamics that leave you drained rather than enriched? It is not uncommon to get caught in a cycle where history seems to repeat itself, drawing you into interactions that feel eerily reminiscent of past toxic connections. This chapter is about breaking that cycle. Here, we will explore how cultivating a deep sense of self-awareness can be your most reliable compass in navigating away from potentially toxic relationships and toward healthier, more fulfilling interactions.

9.1 Self-Awareness and Relationship Patterns

Identifying Personal Relationship Patterns

Reflecting on your past relationships is akin to unfolding a map of your emotional journey—where you have been can significantly inform where you're heading. Often, patterns in our relationships serve as clues to underlying emotional scripts. Are you consistently the caretaker, or perhaps always the one who compromises? Maybe you find yourself drawn to partners who need 'fixing.' Recognizing these patterns is the first step toward understanding the roles you unconsciously adopt.

This recognition is not about casting judgment on yourself; it is about gaining insight into your relational dynamics. For instance, if you notice a pattern of partnering with individuals who take more than they give, this could be a cue to examine your boundaries and self-worth. Each relationship you have experienced holds valuable lessons on what dynamics serve you well and which ones detract from your well-being.

Understanding Personal Triggers

Each of us carries certain vulnerabilities—triggers that, when hit, can sway us into less-than-ideal situations. These triggers often stem from unmet needs or unresolved issues, such as a fear of loneliness, a craving for validation, or the remnants of past traumas. By identifying what specifically makes you vulnerable to toxic relationships, you can begin to develop strategies to fortify yourself in those areas.

For example, if a fear of loneliness propels you into quickly deepening relationships without fully understanding the person, recognizing this can help you pause and reevaluate your pace in future interactions. Understanding your triggers is about self-protection and knowing where your emotional security system needs bolstering to prevent future breaches.

Role of Self-Awareness in Prevention

Increased self-awareness acts as a shield, guarding against the entanglements of toxic relationships. It enables you to recognize the early warning signs and intuit when dynamics do not align with your values or needs. Think of self-awareness as the watchtower from which you can see the approach of potential troubles long before they reach your gates.

Developing this level of awareness requires both introspection and the willingness to learn from each interaction. It asks that you become an observer of your own life, noticing how different interactions make you feel and reflecting on why that may be. This ongoing practice helps solidify your understanding of what healthy relationships look like for you and, very importantly, how they make you feel.

Use of Journals and Therapy for Insight

Journaling and therapy are invaluable tools in enhancing self-awareness. Keeping a relationship journal allows you to document interactions and reflect on them. Over time, patterns emerge, and insights surface. Writing down your feelings and experiences helps externalize them, making it easier to examine and understand them without judgment.

Therapy, on the other hand, provides a structured environment where you can explore your emotions and patterns with professional guidance. Therapists can help you connect dots that might not be obvious, offering strategies to change detrimental relational patterns. They can guide you through the process of understanding and healing from past wounds, which is often necessary to prevent the recurrence of toxic dynamics.

Reflective Journaling Exercise

Consider starting a relationship journal. After each significant interaction, take a moment to jot down:

- How you felt during the interaction.
- What was said or done that evoked these feelings.
- Any reminders of past relationships this interaction may trigger.

This practice not only aids in developing greater self-awareness but also serves as a real-time feedback mechanism for assessing the health of your interactions. It encourages a habit of mindful reflection, deepening your understanding of your relational patterns and triggers, which is essential for cultivating healthier future relationships.

Fostering this enhanced self-awareness equips you with the knowledge and insights necessary to steer clear of potential toxicities and gravitate towards nurturing balanced, and supportive relationships. This proactive approach improves your relational dynamics and contributes significantly to your overall emotional and psychological well-being.

9.2 Choosing the Right Partner: Qualities to Look For

Navigating the landscape of new relationships often feels like trying to read a map without clear landmarks. Knowing which qualities to value in a potential partner can provide much-needed clarity and direction. Key attributes such as empathy, honesty, respect, and emotional stability are not just desirable traits; they are foundational to any healthy and enduring relationship.

Empathy allows a partner to understand and share your feelings, creating a deep emotional connection that enhances mutual support. An empathetic partner can truly put themselves in your shoes, adding a layer of depth and understanding to the relationship that goes beyond surface-level interactions.

Honesty, too, is vital. It fosters trust and openness, making you feel secure and valued in the relationship. When both partners are committed to truthfulness, it eliminates much of the guesswork and insecurity that can plague relationships. This transparency is a cornerstone of intimacy, as it assures you that both the joys and challenges within the relationship are navigated with sincerity. Respect is another non-negotiable quality. It ensures that each person's boundaries are acknowledged and valued, which is crucial for maintaining individuality and personal growth within the partnership. A respectful partner acknowledges your right to your feelings, opinions, and friends, and they will engage with you in discussions and disagreements with courtesy and consideration.

Emotional stability is equally important, as it influences the overall tone and resilience of the relationship. A partner who manages their emotions effectively can handle life's inevitable ups and downs without overreacting or retreating. Such stability fosters a predictable and comforting relationship environment where you feel safe and supported rather than on edge or overly responsible for your partner's emotional well-being.

Understanding the difference between red flags and green flags during the early stages of a relationship can profoundly impact your relationship choices. Red flags, such as lack of communication, disrespect for boundaries, or inconsistent behavior, signal potential problems that might not be resolvable and could lead to emotional pain. In contrast, green flags like consistent respect, open communication, and emotional generosity suggest a healthy, supportive partnership. Recognizing these signs can help you make informed decisions about whether to deepen the relationship or steer clear, potentially saving you from future discord.

The alignment of core values and life goals between partners is another critical aspect of a healthy relationship. Shared values create a strong foundation for mutual understanding and future planning. Whether it is views on family, career ambitions, or personal values like honesty and kindness, alignment in these areas can facilitate smoother interactions and fewer conflicts. When life goals are in sync, it allows both partners to support each other's growth and successes, creating a teamwork dynamic that is both fulfilling and uplifting.

Taking the time to truly know someone before making serious commitments is perhaps one of the most practical pieces of advice for forming lasting relationships. This slow progression allows you to see how your partner handles different situations, including stress, disagreements, and their interactions with others, which are all indicators of their true character. Rushing into commitments can often lead to overlooking potential red flags or misjudging compatibility. Allowing relationships to develop gradually gives both partners time to evaluate their feelings and the relationship dynamics without pressure, ensuring that any commitments made are based on a thorough understanding of each other's personalities, habits, and values.

Understanding these aspects of relationship dynamics encourages a mindful approach to dating and partnerships. It empowers you to make choices based not just on immediate chemistry but on more profound, more sustainable factors that will influence your relationship satisfaction and resilience over time. Focusing on these key qualities and taking a measured approach to your relationships set the stage for healthier, more fulfilling partnerships that can stand the test of time.

9.3 The Power of Healthy Friendships

In the tapestry of your social life, friendships play a crucial and often undervalued role in shaping and supporting your romantic endeavors. Imagine your circle of friends as a garden—each friend a different kind of flower, adding to the garden's diversity and vibrancy. Just as a well-tended garden provides a sanctuary of peace and beauty, strong, healthy friendships offer a safe space for emotional support and honest feedback, which are crucial for nurturing personal growth and maintaining perspective in romantic relationships.

Friendships, especially those that are supportive and respectful, act as a soundboard for your thoughts and feelings about romantic relationships. These relationships provide a mirror, reflecting not just what you present but also what you may not see. For instance, a friend might observe that you seem less joyful or more anxious in your current romantic relationship compared to previous ones. Such observations, coming from a place of care and concern, can help you see patterns you might overlook when swayed by romantic emotions. Friends who know you well understand your personality and values; they can recognize when you might be compromising too much or losing yourself in a relationship. This external perspective is invaluable, especially when your own view might be clouded by affection or desire.

Moreover, the type of friendships you cultivate can significantly influence your romantic relationship choices. Friends who prioritize respect and kindness in their own relationships set a standard and model behaviors that you might aspire to replicate in your romantic life. Conversely, suppose your close friends are frequently engaged in toxic dynamics. In that case, it might normalize such interactions for you, making it harder to recognize and reject similar patterns in your own romantic relationships. Therefore, actively choosing friends who embody and encourage healthy relationship practices can inspire you to expect and demand the same in your love life, steering you away from potential toxicity.

Building and maintaining these healthy friendships requires effort and intentionality, much like romantic relationships. It starts with choosing to connect with individuals who respect your boundaries, support your endeavors, and encourage your happiness. Cultivating such friendships involves regular communication, mutual respect, and a willingness to confront and resolve conflicts constructively. Remember, a true friend seeks your well-being and growth, not compliance or dependency. As you nurture these friendships, you create a reciprocal dynamic where both parties feel valued and supported, establishing a solid network of individuals that enhances all areas of your life.

Encouraging honest feedback from your friends about your relationship choices can significantly impact your romantic life, especially in the early stages of a relationship. This feedback, however, is only as valuable as the honesty and trust established within these friendships. Cultivating an environment where open and candid discussions are welcomed and not judged ensures you can receive and utilize this feedback effectively. It is about creating a safe space where friends feel comfortable sharing their true thoughts, even if they might be hard to hear. Such honest dialogues can help you identify red flags or reaffirm your positive feelings about a new relationship, guiding your decisions with clarity and confidence.

In summary, the relationships you hold with friends are more than just social engagements—they are a foundational support system that shapes your approach to love and life. By investing in friendships rooted in mutual respect and open communication, you fortify your emotional health and gain allies who will cheer you on as you navigate the complexities of romantic relationships. These friendships enrich your life and provide the clarity and support necessary to make informed, healthy romantic choices, ultimately enhancing your overall happiness and well-being.

9.4 Social and Emotional Intelligence in Relationships

Navigating the complexities of human relationships demands more than just good intentions or a friendly disposition. It requires a deep understanding of both social and emotional intelligence—skills that are essential in fostering healthy, meaningful interactions. Social intelligence refers to the ability to effectively navigate and negotiate complex social relationships and environments. In contrast, emotional intelligence is the capacity to be aware of, control, and express one's emotions and to handle interpersonal relationships judicially and empathetically. Together, these forms of intelligence form the backbone of your relational success, influencing how well you connect with others, resolve conflicts, and maintain your personal well-being amid the dynamics of your relational interactions.

Improving your emotional intelligence begins with a commitment to self-awareness. This involves more than just recognizing your emotions as they occur; it also requires understanding the triggers behind these emotions and their impact on your thoughts and actions. For instance, if you find yourself feeling anxious during conflicts, digging deeper to uncover the source of this anxiety can help you address the underlying issues, be it past trauma or a lack of confidence in your conflict-resolution skills. Similarly, developing the ability to recognize and understand the emotions of others is crucial. This empathy allows you to foresee potential conflicts or misunderstandings and navigate these situations with sensitivity and tact, which is invaluable in maintaining healthy relationships.

Another critical aspect of emotional intelligence is the management of emotions. This does not mean suppressing your feelings but rather understanding the appropriate times and ways to express them. Effective emotional management helps you respond to situations rather than reacting impulsively, enabling you to handle relational dynamics more smoothly and reduce potential conflicts. For example, if you are feeling overwhelmed by anger, knowing how to pause and process this emotion can prevent a heated argument and allow for a more constructive discussion later. Practicing techniques such as deep breathing, mindfulness, or even temporary disengagement can aid in managing intense emotions and preserving your relationships and mental health.

Social skills are equally integral to relationship building. Effective communication is at the heart of this, involving the words you choose and your tone, timing, and body language. Active listening plays a pivotal role here—it is about fully concentrating on what is being said rather than just passively hearing the message. This skill ensures that you understand the perspective of others, which fosters mutual respect and minimizes misunderstandings. Conflict resolution skills are also essential, as conflicts are inevitable in any relationship. Being able to approach disagreements with a problem-solving attitude rather than a combative stance can transform conflicts from relationship roadblocks into opportunities for growth and deeper understanding.

The ability to read and interpret social cues is another facet of social intelligence that can significantly influence your interactions. These cues, which can be as subtle as a change in tone or as evident as a facial expression, provide insight into the emotional state and comfort levels of those around you. Being attuned to these signals allows you to adjust your behavior and responses appropriately, enhancing your interactions and helping to maintain harmony within your relationships.

Applying these social and emotional intelligence skills is particularly effective in avoiding toxic relationships. By understanding your own emotional landscape and that of others, you can quickly identify behaviors that may signal manipulative or harmful intentions. For example, if you notice that someone consistently invalidates your feelings or ignores your boundaries, recognizing these as red flags can prompt you to reevaluate the relationship's health. Similarly, strong social skills enable you to set and communicate your boundaries clearly, reducing the risk of being drawn into dynamics that are disrespectful or detrimental.

Moreover, the combination of keen emotional insight and robust social strategies empowers you to foster relationships that are not only supportive and respectful but also enriching. It allows you to build connections that are based on mutual understanding and genuine care, which are the hallmarks of any healthy relationship. By continuously developing your social and emotional intelligence, you equip yourself with the tools to navigate the complexities of human relationships and enrich these interactions, creating a network of support and affection that enhances every aspect of your life.

9.5 Continuous Self-Growth and Relationship Health

The path to maintaining vibrant and healthy relationships is intricately tied to your personal growth and development. It is much like tending a garden; just as a garden requires ongoing attention and nurturing to thrive, so do your relationships benefit from continuous personal growth. Engaging in lifelong learning and actively pursuing personal development is about acquiring new skills or expanding knowledge and transforming these experiences into insights that enhance your relational dynamics.

Imagine personal growth as a journey where each new skill learned or insight gained acts as a stepping stone, leading to more informed and mature relationship choices. For instance, learning how to manage stress effectively improves your personal well-being and enhances your interactions with others, making you a more patient and understanding partner, friend, or colleague. Each book read, each seminar attended, and each reflection period spent in understanding yourself better equips you with tools to build stronger, more resilient relationships. These tools help you navigate the complexities of human emotions and interactions with greater ease and confidence, thereby reducing the likelihood of falling into toxic relationship patterns.

Moreover, pursuing personal hobbies and interests plays a crucial role in this developmental journey. Engaging in activities you are passionate about enriches your life and bolsters your self-esteem and independence. These pursuits provide a healthy outlet for stress, enhance your life satisfaction, and cultivate a sense of accomplishment. All these factors contribute to a stronger sense of self, which is essential in establishing and maintaining healthy relationships. When you are confident in your abilities and satisfied with your endeavors, you are less likely to seek validation from relationships, thereby reducing the risk of codependency.

Furthermore, hobbies often introduce you to new social circles and opportunities for interaction, expanding your understanding of different perspectives and enhancing your interpersonal skills. This exposure can be incredibly beneficial in broadening your horizons and fostering empathy, a key component of emotional intelligence that is vital in all forms of relationships. Having empathy for another individual is the ability to understand another person's situation or feelings.

The assessment and adjustment of relationship goals and expectations is another area where continuous self-growth plays a vital role. Relationships evolve over time, as do the individuals within them. Regularly taking stock of your relationship goals and aligning them with your personal growth ensures that your relationships do not stagnate or veer off into directions that no longer align with your values or life aspirations. This might mean redefining what you seek in a partner as you grow older, or it could involve setting new boundaries that reflect your current needs and desires. For example, as you advance in your career, you might prioritize a partner who understands and supports your professional commitments, adjusting your relationship dynamics to include more support for career-related activities.

This dynamic reassessment keeps your relationships fresh and aligned with your personal growth and ensures that they remain fulfilling and supportive over time. It encourages a mutual evolution, where both partners grow both individually and as a couple, adapting to each life stage with flexibility and resilience.

By embracing a philosophy of lifelong learning and continuous self-improvement, you equip yourself with the tools necessary to cultivate and maintain healthy, fulfilling relationships. This proactive personal and relational growth approach fosters a life rich in love, understanding, and mutual respect.

As we conclude this exploration of preventative strategies to avoid toxic relationships, it becomes clear that the journey toward healthier relational dynamics is deeply intertwined with our personal development. Each strategy discussed in this chapter—from cultivating self-awareness to enhancing social and emotional intelligence—serves as a testament to the power of personal growth in shaping our relationship choices.

In the next chapter, we will explore how we can apply mindfulness principles to enhance our relationship dynamics, offering practical techniques and insights to help us remain present and engaged in our interactions with others. This continuation is about maintaining the status quo and actively enriching our relationships through mindful awareness and presence, ensuring that each connection we foster is as healthy and fulfilling as possible.

CHAPTER 10
EMPOWERING YOURSELF
AND OTHERS

Have you ever felt a ripple of change that begins with a single, simple action? Imagine that action stemming from your own dedication to fostering healthy relationships, not just in your personal life but extending outward into your community. This chapter is about transforming personal growth into a broader mission—becoming an advocate for healthy relationship dynamics. It is about taking your understanding and broadcasting it wider, turning personal insights into public action. By promoting awareness and education, you can play a crucial part in altering how relationships are viewed and handled by those around you.

10.1 Becoming an Advocate for Healthy Relationships

Role As An Advocate

Being an advocate for healthy relationships means more than just understanding what makes a relationship flourish—it is about actively promoting these principles and educating others. It involves being a voice that challenges the norms of toxic relationships and highlights the features of supportive, nurturing partnerships. Your role extends beyond your personal experiences; it encompasses influencing others through education, support, and leadership. This advocacy can take place in various arenas of your life—from your home and social circles to broader community platforms. The essence of advocacy lies in the commitment to spread knowledge and support others in their quest for healthier relationships, making it a powerful tool for societal change.

Educational Outreach

One effective way to advocate for healthier relationships is through educational outreach. This can be achieved in several ways, such as organizing workshops, participating in speaking events, or even writing about your experiences and insights on blogs or social media platforms. Each platform offers a unique way to engage with different audiences. For instance, workshops can provide a direct and interactive way to teach people about relationship dynamics, offering practical advice and strategies. Speaking at events can help reach a broader audience, inspiring others with your story and valuable knowledge. Meanwhile, writing provides a more personal touch, allowing you to delve deep into your journey and the lessons learned, which can resonate with those experiencing similar challenges. Each method helps spread crucial information and positions you as a knowledgeable figure in the realm of relationship health.

Collaboration With Organizations

To amplify your impact, consider collaborating with local organizations, schools, or support groups focusing on relationship health. These partnerships can significantly extend the reach of your advocacy efforts, enabling you to influence a larger and more diverse audience. Organizations often have access to resources and networks that can help disseminate information more effectively. For example, teaming up with a local school to integrate relationship education into their curriculum can equip young people with the knowledge they need to form healthy relationships from an early age. Similarly, working with support groups can provide resources and platforms to share your insights with those actively seeking help. These collaborations not only broaden the scope of your impact but also enhance the credibility and depth of the information shared, creating a more substantial effect on the community's approach to relationships.

Personal Empowerment Through Advocacy

While advocacy focuses on educating and supporting others, it also offers significant personal benefits. Engaging in advocacy reinforces your own understanding of healthy relationships and deepens your commitment to these principles. It is a dynamic process where teaching others reinforces and expands your insights, creating a continuous loop of learning and growth. Moreover, advocacy can be incredibly empowering, providing a sense of purpose and achievement. Knowing that your efforts are helping others escape or improve toxic relationship patterns can be profoundly fulfilling. It transforms personal pain into a powerful catalyst for change, both in your life and in the lives of others.

Interactive Element: Reflection Section

To further integrate these concepts, reflect on how you can begin or enhance your role as an advocate for healthy relationships. Consider the following questions:

- What platforms or opportunities are available in your community for sharing knowledge about healthy relationships?
- How can you collaborate with local organizations or groups to extend your reach?
- In what ways can advocating for healthier relationships enrich your personal journey toward healing and growth?

Reflecting on these questions can help you identify practical steps to advance your advocacy efforts, turning your knowledge and experiences into tools for broader societal change. Whether you choose to lead workshops, write articles, or collaborate with community organizations, each action you take contributes to a larger movement towards healthier relationships. By stepping into the role of an advocate, you not only empower others but also reinforce your own journey of growth and healing, making a lasting impact that extends far beyond your own experiences.

10.2 Sharing Your Journey: When and How to Help Others

Sharing your personal experiences with toxic relationships is not just about recounting your past; it is about offering a beacon of hope to others who might be navigating similar tumultuous waters. Deciding when and how to share your story is pivotal—it requires a keen sense of empathy and timing to ensure that your message is both heard and helpful. It is essential to consider the readiness of your audience. Are they at a point in their recovery where your story could inspire hope rather than trigger pain? Gauging this can be challenging, but signs like seeking advice, sharing their experiences, or asking questions about your growth can indicate readiness. The setting also plays a crucial role; a quiet, private environment might encourage more open and heartfelt discussions than a public or less intimate one.

When it comes to methods of sharing, each carries its unique set of benefits and challenges. One-on-one conversations can provide a personal touch and allow for deep connection, making it easier to tailor your story to the listener's needs. However, this method can also be emotionally draining, as it requires a lot of emotional output and can sometimes lead to over-sharing. Public speaking, whether at events or workshops, allows you to reach a broader audience and can be highly empowering. This method can help solidify your own understanding and commitment to your healing path. However, it lacks the personalization of one-on-one interactions and may require different skills to ensure the audience is engaged and can relate to your message. Whether through blogs, books, or articles, writing offers a reflective way to share your journey. It allows you to articulate your thoughts and experiences carefully and can be therapeutic. The challenge here is ensuring your written words convey the emotions and lessons as powerfully as they are felt.

The impact of sharing your journey can be profound. For those who hear or read your story, it can act as a validation of their own experiences. It can make them feel seen and understood and, importantly, not alone. This can be incredibly empowering. Knowing that someone else has navigated similar challenges and has come out stronger on the other side can provide hope and motivation.

Additionally, it can also inspire them to seek help or begin their own process of healing. For you, sharing can reinforce your growth and healing. It serves as a reminder of how far you have come and fortifies your resilience against potential future challenges.

However, setting boundaries around how and what you share is crucial. Protecting your emotional well-being is paramount. Decide in advance how much detail you are comfortable sharing, and be prepared to steer the conversation away from areas that might be too raw or personal. Recognize signs of emotional drain —feelings of fatigue, discomfort, or sadness during or after sharing—and give yourself permission to step back and replenish your emotional reserves. This might mean taking a break from sharing for a period or choosing methods of sharing that are less emotionally taxing. Remember, sharing your story is about helping others and continuing to nurture your well-being and growth.

10.3 Celebrating Independence and Interdependence in Relationships

Navigating the delicate balance between independence and inter-dependence is akin to walking a tightrope. Too much of one can lead to a loss of self or a lack of unity. In relationships, it is crucial to foster a balance where both partners can enjoy their personal freedoms while actively contributing to their shared life. This equilibrium enhances the relationship's dynamics and enriches each individual's personal growth.

Independence in a relationship means having the space to be yourself, pursue your own interests, and maintain your unique identity outside the relationship. It is about having the freedom to make choices and enjoy aspects of life independently of your partner. Celebrating this independence involves recognizing and supporting each other's achievements and goals. For instance, you might take time to acknowledge your partner's professional accomplishments or support them as they pursue a personal hobby. It is also vital to set individual goals, whether they pertain to career aspirations, fitness targets, or educational endeavors. These objectives foster personal growth and can bring a sense of accomplishment and fulfillment that is entirely your own. Maintaining personal hobbies and interests is equally important. These activities provide a healthy outlet for stress and enrich your sense of self, which you then bring back into the relationship, keeping the partnership vibrant and dynamic.

On the flip side, interdependence involves a mutual dependence where both partners rely on each other's strengths to create a stronger, unified partnership. It is about building a relationship where both individuals feel secure, supported, and connected, knowing they can count on each other. Fostering healthy interdependence can be achieved through joint decision-making, where both partners have an equal say in decisions that affect their shared lives. This practice reinforces respect and equality and strengthens communication and Trust. Mutual support in personal growth is another cornerstone of interdependence. Encouraging and celebrating each other's development, whether professional, personal, or emotional, reinforces the partnership's foundation. Shared responsibilities are also integral, whether managing household tasks, parenting, or supporting each other during challenging times. This shared load not only eases individual burdens but also deepens the bond by working together toward common goals.

Acknowledging and appreciating each partner's contributions is crucial in maintaining the balance between independence and interdependence. This recognition should extend beyond tangible tasks to include emotional support, patience, understanding, and encouragement. Regularly expressing gratitude for these contributions fosters a positive atmosphere and highlights the value of each partner's role in the relationship. It is about seeing and appreciating the whole person, recognizing their efforts in both the relationship and their personal achievements.

In essence, the dance between independence and interdependence in relationships is about creating a partnership where both individuals feel valued, supported, and connected, yet free to be themselves. It is a dynamic balance that requires ongoing attention and adjustment, but when achieved, it forms the basis of a strong, healthy, and resilient relationship. Celebrating personal freedoms and shared bonds within your relationship creates a nurturing environment that encourages individual and collective growth, ensuring you and your partner flourish together.

As we wrap up this chapter, remember that the strength of a relationship often lies in its ability to adapt to the needs of both partners. Balancing independence and interdependence allows you and your partner to grow both individually and together, creating a partnership that is both supportive and freeing. In this book, we have learned that by recognizing the signs of toxic relationships, applying strategies to maintain your strong sense of self, setting boundaries for self-protection, and working together with a dedicated individual, you can obtain healthy, supportive relationships in both your intimate relationships as well as developing strong, supportive friendships.

CONCLUSION: EMBRACING FREEDOM AND BUILDING HEALTHIER FUTURES

In concluding our journey toward freedom from toxic relationships, it is essential to reflect on the transformative power of recognizing and addressing gaslighting, narcissism, and codependency. This book aims to provide practical, stress-free steps to identify these harmful dynamics and equip you with the tools necessary to rebuild your self-worth and develop healthier relationships.

Understanding and recognizing red flags early on is crucial in preventing toxic relationships from taking root. By honing your awareness and practicing mindfulness, you can create a protective barrier against manipulative behaviors and ensure that you remain grounded in your truth. Mindfulness allows you to stay present, observe your thoughts and emotions without judgment, and make conscious decisions that align with your well-being.

Rebuilding self-worth after experiencing toxic relationships is a gradual and deeply personal process. Remember, it is not just about avoiding negative influences but also about fostering positive, nurturing connections that support your growth. Embrace the journey of self-discovery, acknowledging your strengths and learning from past experiences. Every step you take toward self-compassion and resilience reinforces your ability to form and maintain healthy relationships.

If you have tried before and found the path challenging, take heart. Progress is rarely linear, and setbacks are a natural part of growth. Each attempt brings you closer to understanding yourself and your needs better. Be patient with yourself and recognize that healing is an ongoing journey, not a destination.

As you move forward, keep these fundamental principles in mind:

1. **Self-Awareness:** Continuously cultivate an awareness of your thoughts, feelings, and behaviors. This self-awareness will help you identify when you might be slipping into old patterns and empower you to make healthier choices.
2. **Boundaries:** Establish and maintain clear boundaries to protect your emotional and mental well-being. Healthy relationships are built on mutual respect and understanding; boundaries are essential for fostering that respect.
3. **Support Systems:** Surround yourself with a supportive network of friends, family, or professional counselors who can provide guidance and encouragement. Do not hesitate to seek help when needed.
4. **Ongoing Learning:** Commit to ongoing personal development. Stay curious about yourself and your relationships, and be open to learning new strategies for maintaining health and happiness.
5. **Self-Compassion:** Treat yourself with kindness and understanding.

Acknowledge your efforts and progress, no matter how small they may seem. Self-compassion is a vital component of healing and building resilience.

By implementing these strategies and maintaining a mindful approach to your relationships, you can break free from the cycle of toxicity and move toward a life filled with genuine connections and inner peace. Embrace your journey with courage and optimism, knowing that each step you take is a powerful affirmation of your commitment to a healthier, more fulfilling future.

Remember, the journey to freedom and healthy relationships is ongoing, and every effort you make is a testament to your strength and resilience. Here's to a future where you thrive in relationships that uplift and empower you.

KEEPING THE GAME ALIVE

Now you have everything you need to break free from toxic relationships and reclaim your happiness, it is time to pass on your newfound knowledge and show other readers where they can find the same help.

Simply by leaving your honest opinion of this book on Amazon, you will show other readers who are struggling with toxic relationships where they can find the information theyre looking for, and pass their passion for healthy, supportive connections forward.

Thank you for your help. The journey to freedom from toxic relationships is kept alive when we pass on our knowledge – and you are helping me to do just that.

Simply scan the QR code below to leave your review:

REFERENCES

Toxic Relationships: The Experiences and Effects ... https://www.ncbi.nlm.nih.gov/pmc/articles/PMC9527357/

Gaslighting Examples and How to Respond https://www.verywellmind.com/gaslighting-examples-7567491

How to Stop Being Codependent: 9 Tips to Overcome It https://www.talkspace.com/blog/how-to-stop-being-codependent/

Five Ways to Heal Your Self-Esteem After Leaving an Abusive Relationship https://cptsdfoundation.org/2022/11/29/five-ways-to-heal-your-self-esteem-after-leaving-an-abusive-relationship/

Gaslighting: Signs and Tips for Seeking Help https://www.healthline.com/health/gaslighting

Cultivating Self-Love to Heal Codependency - Kripalu https://kripalu.org/resources/cultivating-self-love-heal-codependency

Toxic Relationships: How to Let Go When It's Unhappily ... https://www.heysigmund.com/toxic-relationship-how-to-let-go/

How to Be Assertive and Set Healthy Boundaries https://welldoing.org/article/how-be-assertive-set-healthy-boundaries

Healing After Emotional Abuse: A Therapist's Guide https://www.talkspace.com/blog/healing-after-emotional-abuse/

Mindfulness-based treatments for posttraumatic stress disorder https://www.ncbi.nlm.nih.gov/pmc/articles/PMC5747539/

Learning to Trust After an Abusive Relationship https://www.psychologytoday.com/us/blog/invisible-bruises/202204/learning-to-trust-after-an-abusive-relationship

5 Powerful Self-Care Tips for Abuse and Trauma Survivors https://www.thehotline.org/resources/5-powerful-self-care-tips-for-abuse-and-trauma-survivors/

Healing Emotional Abuse With Self-Kindness https://www.psychologytoday.com/us/blog/the-compassion-chronicles/202110/healing-emotional-abuse-self-kindness

Personal Goal Setting - Planning to Live Your Life Your Way https://www.mindtools.com/a5ykiuq/personal-goal-setting

50 Powerful Positive Affirmations to Break Free From Toxic ... https://spiritualprimate.com/50-powerful-positive-affirmations-to-break-free-from-toxic-relationships/

A Success Story: She Found Love After Leaving A Toxic Relationship https://toddcreager.com/a-success-story-she-found-love-after-leaving-a-toxic-relationship/

How to Be Emotionally Intelligent in Love Relationships https://www.helpguide.org/arti cles/mental-health/emotional-intelligence-love-relationships.htm

7 Effective Communication Techniques for Strengthening Your Relationship https://raft consulting.com/blog/11869/7-Effective-Communication-Techniques-for-Strengthening-Your-Relationship

Conflict Resolution in Relationships & Couples: 5 Strategies https://positivepsychology. com/conflict-resolution-relationships/

The Concept of Individuality in a Relationship and Why it is Essential https://theon linetherapist.blog/the-concept-of-individuality-in-a-relationship-and-why-it-is-essential/

How to Set Healthy Boundaries in Relationships https://www.helpguide.org/articles/ relationships-communication/setting-healthy-boundaries-in-relationships.htm

Setting Healthy Boundaries in Relationships https://www.helpguide.org/articles/rela tionships-communication/setting-healthy-boundaries-in-relationships.htm

How to Deal with People Who Repeatedly Violate Your Boundaries https://psychcentral. com/blog/imperfect/2016/07/how-to-deal-with-people-who-repeatedly-violate-your-boundaries

Self-Care: The Key to Breaking Free from Toxic Relationships https://movingbeyondyou. org/self-care-the-key-to-breaking-free-from-toxic-relationships/

How to Leave an Abusive Relationship Safely https://www.verywellmind.com/making-a-safety-plan-to-escape-abusive-relationship-5069959

Rebuilding Your Finances After Financial Abuse https://www.bankrate.com/personal-finance/rebuild-finances-after-financial-abuse/

How to Perform Assertiveness Training: 6 Exercises https://positivepsychology.com/ assertiveness-training/

National Domestic Violence Hotline: Domestic Violence Support https://www.thehot line.org/

13 signs you're emotionally ready for a relationship https://www.businessinsider.com/ how-to-know-if-youre-ready-for-a-relationship-2018-11

How to Build Trust in a Relationship, According to a Therapist https://www.verywell mind.com/how-to-build-trust-in-a-relationship-5207611

18 Relationship Red Flags: Examples, Signs and What to Do https://www.today.com/life/ relationships/relationship-red-flags-rcna52755

The Role of Therapy in Building Healthy Relationships https://care-clinics.com/the-role-of-therapy-in-building-healthy-relationships/

How long should I wait for him to ask me out? 4 important tips - Hack Spirit. https:// hackspirit.com/how-long-should-wait-him-ask-me-out/

Meet BMind, the Revolutionary AI-Powered Smart Mirror Unveiled at #CES2024" – Smart Tech Shopping. https://smarttechshopping.com/blogs/news/the-revolution ary-ai-powered-smart-mirror

Addressing Inappropriate Behavior: How to Handle Uncomfortable Situations with a Young Relative. https://sanukinosato-eng.com/amp/addressing-inappropriate-behavior-how-to-handle-uncomfortable-situations-with-a-young-relative

Managing Family - THERAPY WITH STEPHANIE BAIN. https://www.stephaniebaintherapy.com/blog/my-3-part-framework-for-managing-family-relationships

JAMB UTME Exam Anxiety: Coping Strategies for a Stress-Free Experience - JAMB Past Questions. https://www.supergb.com/cbt/users/journal/article/521d0483-5ccf-4803-8dfd-dd17df82ff85

8 Things Men Secretly Want Their Partners To Do. https://beautyhealthpage.com/8-things-men-secretly-want-their-partners-to-do/

OpenAI. (2024). *ChatGPT (4o)* [Large language model]. https://chatgpt.com

Effective Communication | The Better Institute. https://betterinstitute.com/blog-effective-communication/

Made in the USA
Las Vegas, NV
10 January 2025

16163275R00083